The
SHELTER

God's Rescue Of The Abused

ELLIS

www.xulonpress.com

Acknowledgements

My heart is full of gratefulness to God
Who has brought me into a new fullness of life
Through His healing process.
I dedicate this book to all the dear people
Who have suffered because of abuse.
May God continue to bring healing to your soul
As you earnestly seek Him.

I want to also acknowledge a dear friend,
(remaining anonymous)
Who found an escape from domestic abuse
And earnestly studied the Scriptures with me
to learn God's ways.

She also tirelessly edited every page,
and helped to smooth out the rough places.

I am grateful to Almighty God
For faithful friends who never fail.

Table of Contents

Introduction

This is not a book to read once and then donate to Goodwill. For those who have suffered and endured domestic abuse, this devotional is one to read over, and over, and over again. God can heal you from the assaults of domestic abuse, but it may take a passage of time to feel "cured." That word, "cured," to me is a relative term. I don't feel completely "cured," but I am a lot more peaceful than I once was. I have a better grip on who I am, what my priorities in life are, and what my goals in life consist of. Simply put, I have a better handle on ME!

The secular world can help to build a fortress of safety for those attempting to escape domestic abuse. I was given a lot of worldly advice: get a restraining order, stay in a "safe place," call 9-1-1 if threatened, look both ways when entering and exiting a building, keep your doors locked with a peephole to observe who is there, keep your phone charged, keep your car keys in sight, take threats seriously.

These are truly words of wisdom and are valid for physical protection and safety. But what about your emotions, your understandings, your self-image, your spirit, your confidence, your feelings of stability?

Domestic abuse is more than damage to your body. Your body may have been wounded, but it can heal. The deepest slaughter may be in your heart, in your soul, in your deepest being. What is sadly missing in the process of recovering from years of abuse is some "heart healing." The world may offer a Band-Aid, a shelter in a "safe place," monetary support to buy gas and groceries, rent assistance, legal advice. But you may ask, "What about my crushed spirit?"

Persistent rage and violence from an abuser can wound the human spirit and even take a human life. The effects of a physical attack (bruises, stitches, broken bones) can heal, sometimes after one trip to the emergency room. But the emotional, psychological and spiritual wounds may take years to heal as abuse attacks the deepest part of your personhood. Abuse makes you feel like a Nobody. You pulled alongside another person, with love and trust, openness and intimacy, only to learn that these attributes were truthfully never reciprocated with your partner. In fact, your trust in him was ripped to shreds, leaving you feeling emotionally assaulted and abandoned, bruised and bloody, discarded as in the trash. You are petrified to think about the answer to the question, "Does he love me?" Or even worse, "Did he ever love me?"

It seems like endless confusion has taken over. How can you lift your head again? How can you restore your broken and mangled personhood? Where can you turn to find healing for your innermost being? Where is the doctor who can stitch the heart? Is anybody listening to me?

This book is an effort to seek healing for our entire being—physically, emotionally, cognitively, spiritually. God is the ultimate Healer. He made us. He knows us. He alone can reach the heart. Jesus shows how He heals after a tender touch of His garment by an infirm woman.

"As Jesus was on his way, the crowds almost crushed him.

*And a woman was there
who had been subject to bleeding for twelve years,
but no one could heal her.*

*She came up behind him and touched the edge of his cloak,
and immediately her bleeding stopped.
'Who touched me?' Jesus asked.
When they all denied it, Peter said,*

*'Master, the people are crowding and pressing against you.'
But Jesus said, 'Someone touched me;
I know that power has gone out from me.'*

*Then the woman, seeing that she could not go unnoticed,
came trembling and fell at his feet. In the presence of all the people,
she told why she had touched him and how she had been instantly healed.*

Then he said to her, 'Daughter, your faith has healed you. Go in peace.'"
(Luke 8:42b-48).

What can we learn from this healing?

- This woman was bleeding—for twelve years. From her body, and from her spirit.
- This woman reached out in faith to Jesus—just touching his garment.
- Jesus had the power to heal her completely.
- She came to Him "trembling and fell at his feet."
- This woman was instantly healed.

That's where we need to be. As this woman did, we, too, can come "trembling" and fall at His feet. How can we touch Jesus for healing? That is the purpose of this book. We are going to reach out to touch Jesus, even if it is the last morsel of energy and faith we have. The woman felt "unnoticed." She didn't feel important or worthy. She felt like no one would even notice her as she approached Jesus with her fingertips, in fear and trembling.

Would he see her?

Would he care about her?

Would he, could he, heal her?

Would the bleeding stop?

From firsthand experience, I can say that I felt exactly like this woman. Wounding from the husband of my youth had left me in pieces, not knowing who

I was, or why someone would treat me this way. Why does he hurt me? Why am I bleeding, in my heart? Why do my thoughts swirl around in confusion and despair? Where is God in this picture?

This book is the result of my personal search for answers from God. It is 40 days toward healing of the body, of the mind and of the spirit. And it falls in sequential order with first things first:

I. God Creates

God made me, from the inside to the outside. I am who I am because God made me to be who I am. The environment I was raised in is also His design. None of us have control over our nuclear family, which was part of our molding and can be used of God. He uses who we are, as we are, to make our lives full and purposeful. It ultimately gives the glory back to Him, who is the great Deliverer.

We will learn to realize how special we are in God's eyes. We ARE His creation!

II. God Loves

God is the ultimate source of love. Human love will always have limitations. In an outpouring of His love, God has promised to give us everything we REALLY need. Sometimes we have to adjust our thinking to realize exactly that—what do I REALLY need? The first thing we need is forgiveness from our depravity and sin. We are fallen creatures, sinful and selfish. God sent his son Jesus to die on the cross as a punishment for our sins and a way to find forgiveness and peace from an Almighty God. He truly has done all we need for forgiveness and his ways have offered us the fullest life possible here on earth. That's how much he truly loves us. And He is even more as He cares for our every breath. He says, (emphasis mine) *"Cast ALL your care upon (Me), for (I) care for you"* (I Peter 5:6-8).

We will learn to know and believe that God's love for us is the deepest, the strongest, the purest, the most complete.

III. Abuse Hurts

In a sinful world there will be sinful acts. Abusive acts—physical, verbal, emotional, spiritual—are an effort for one person to control another person. The abuser finds some power and purpose in himself when he has his victim by his side, meeting his every need. This control is spawned from his inward emptiness and lack of self-awareness and confidence. Control makes him feel like he is SOMEBODY. "Just look at me.

Just look at my wife!" But he has no ability or skills to develop a "heart to heart" relationship with her. He blesses her with outward gifts and promises. She also, in her inability to understand the elements of a "heart to heart" relationship, falls easily into his clutches. She blends into HIS life with all its excitement.

Slowly, slowly she loses the inability to REALLY talk with him. She knows she can't share her true feelings. Sadly, what it does to her is destroy who she is. She is forced to become who her abuser wants her to be. He wants her totally for HIS needs. Her needs are secondary, or maybe non-existent. If she questions him or refuses to comply with his desires, the verbal and physical abuse becomes stronger, and it keeps her subservient. With his need to control, and her feelings of weakness within herself, the combination is destructive for both. It becomes a very complex psychological deficiency for both the abuser and the victim. The couple LOOKS like they are in a happy marriage. But the reality is that they are far apart from each other, just going through the motions. What goes on behind closed doors is a sharp contrast to what is seen in public.

In domestic abuse the abuser eventually stoops to evil and hurtful acts to keep the façade going. He becomes jealous, gives her the silent treatment, he does things behind her back, he doesn't communicate (or refuses to communicate) because he wants to run the show. Eventually his anger takes hold with name-calling, loud threats, pounding fists, throwing furniture, hurting pets, slapping her across the face, and even abandonment. All of this is truly SIN.

It is true that murder/suicide incidents can start with domestic abuse. She finally found strength in herself to stand up to the hurts. In her frustration, she may just "want out" and turns to the courts for a restraining order or a divorce. That's when she is in the most danger, and that's when he may snap and end it all, for both of them.

That's why the sin of domestic abuse is serious business! Domestic abuse needs INTERVENTION before it succumbs to death.

We can all agree that the origin of sin is Satan. It is Satan who is in a battle with God and seeks to destroy God's creation. And marriage is God's creation. The author of evil is Satan himself whose purpose is to "*steal, kill and destroy*" (John 10:10) God's creation. His ugly head shows in many forms of abuse.

The Scripture shows us how to define and confront the sinful acts of abuse. God's Word is truly the "*sword of the Spirit*" (Ephesians 6:17), going to the very heart of the sin. His Word gives us armor and is able to offer protection in any assault. Our job is to turn to God, as the woman with the issue of blood did when she reached out to touch his garment for healing. Come out of denial, face the abuse straight on as sin, insist that it stops, expect repentance, seek reconciliation, and live in the light of God's love.

We will learn ways to confront the sin of abuse.

IV. God Forgives

God forgives us, and He leads the way for us to forgive others. Lack of a forgiving spirit only hurts the person who continues to relish in bitterness and vindictive retaliation toward another. Jesus is the center of forgiveness and He gives us the strength to forgive our enemies, even when it seems impossible. In His example of prayer to us, His disciples, He says (emphasis mine):

"Forgive us our (sins), as we forgive those who (sin) against us." (Matthew 6:9-13)

If we fail to forgive, will God forgive us? The Bible says there are devastating results for anyone who refuses to forgive. It actually changes the nature of that person, and this darkness may spill over to others in hurtful ways. Nothing good comes out of a failure to forgive:

"Get rid of all bitterness, rage and anger, brawling and
slander, along with every form of malice.
Be kind and compassionate to one another,
forgiving each other, just as Christ God forgave you."
(Ephesians 4:31-32)

It's a choice He gives us. We can stay with a life filled with bitterness, rage, anger, brawling, slander, and malice; or we can ask God for help to forgive. But what if someone has hurt me in deep ways? How can I forgive? This is when it becomes ultimately important to search out a way to forgive, when it is hard. God offers a way of freedom from inward retaliation toward another, and it all becomes real in the forgiveness offered in Christ.

We will explore the topic of forgiveness, especially when it seems impossible.

V. God Restores

When an abused woman wants to escape the wounding, God will guide her steps. It is not healthy for her or for her abuser to continue to live in a destructive environment. First it is important to find a "safe place" to clear out the cobwebs and learn some healthy thought patterns. God's Word gives clear instructions, and that's what this devotional book is all about. Professionals in domestic abuse therapy can also give needed insight. But the deepest healing comes through reading and applying God's Word. Step by step God will restore and heal. He instructs us first to seek His will:

"Do not conform any longer to the pattern of this world,
but be transformed by the renewing of your mind.
Then you will be able to test and approve what God's
will is—his good, pleasing and perfect will."
(Romans 12:2)

If I could give my perspective on this verse concerning how God can transform our thought patterns, I would enlarge it to say:

"Do not conform any longer to the pattern of this world
(Put a stop to evil behavior),
but be transformed
(Change thinking patterns)

by the renewing of your mind.
(Replace old thinking with new thinking).

Then you will be able to test and approve
(Learn)
*"what God's will is—his good, pleasing and perfect
will."* (Romans 12:2)
(Because living in God's will is the most extraordinary and exciting, full and complete way to live.)

Can God restore us to a life of freedom, fullness and completeness in Him? The answer is, without a doubt, YES. In fact, He can turn all of this suffering into GOOD.

*"And we know that in all things God works for the
good of those who love him, who have been called
according to his purpose."*
(Romans 8:28)

We will cling onto the ways God will restore us to a life of sanity and wholeness.

MY STORY

When I escaped from an abusive environment, I gradually learned, howbeit slowly, that God had greater plans for me. I am now free to live my life without disparaging condemnations, passive (undercover) hurts, slander, helplessness, aloneness, secrecy, deception, threats, entrapment, humiliating slaps, name calling, fear and more. I CHOOSE NOT TO STAY THERE! I made the decision to stand up to the abuse and insist that it ends. Never forget that God gives you all the strength you need:

> *"What, then, shall we say in response to this?*
> *If God is for us, who can be against us?"*
> (Romans 8:31)

Because Jesus was here in the flesh, He knows! He feels! He weeps with us in the face of sin. And he is not a stranger to abuse. In fact, He is truly on the front lines of suffering:

- *"He was despised and rejected by men..."* (Isaiah 53:3)
- *"He was a man of sorrows...* (Isaiah 53:3)
- *"and familiar with suffering:..."* (Isaiah 53:3)
- *"Jesus wept"* (John 11:35)
- *"I offered my back to those who beat me, my cheeks to those who pulled out my beard; I did not hide my face from mocking and spitting."* (Isaiah 50:6)

- *"Then they spit in his face and struck him with their fists. Others slapped him and said, 'Prophesy to us, Christ. Who hit you?'"* (Matthew 26:67)

Yet what was his response to severe wounding, and finally death as he was nailed to the cross?

"Father, forgive them for they know not what they are doing." (Luke 23:24)

Yes, we are told to forgive, which we must do, acknowledging at the same time that something is terribly wrong when a man hurts a woman. Offering forgiveness doesn't mean we need to stand there and get beaten, over and over. We should not enable them, or help them, to continue in the sin of hurting others. Truly they don't know what they are doing! And the Sovereign (or All Knowing) God, amazing as it seems, is the One who is helping with our deliverance:

"Because the Sovereign LORD helps me,
I will not be disgraced.
Therefore I have set my face like flint,
and I know I will not be put to shame.

He who vindicates me is near.
Who then will bring charges against me?
Let us face each other!
Who is my accuser?
Let him confront me!
IT IS THE SOVEREIGN LORD WHO HELPS ME."
(Isaiah 50:7-9)

Meditate on these words from God. Receive your healing. Make them part of your recovery and renewal. Let them fill you with hope and direction as you face the future. Be assured that God is always with you.

"In my anguish I cried to the LORD,
and he answered by setting me free.

The Lord is with me; I will not be afraid.
What can man do to me?

The LORD is with me; he is my helper.
I will look in triumph on my enemies.
It is better to take refuge in the LORD
Than to trust in man."
(Psalm 118:5-8)

God provides our ultimate SHELTER. Nothing temporary. His SHELTER is permanent! All we need to do is turn to Him. He will be there.

There are 40 devotional readings in this book to take us on a healing journey away from domestic abuse and into the Light of God's love and protection. Read on your own, or read with a group, and start on your adventure toward wholeness.

Defining Abuse

"You, my brothers, were called to be free.
But do not use your freedom as an opportunity for
self-indulgence;
Rather, serve one another in love.
The entire law is summed up in a single command:
'Love your neighbor as yourself.'
If you keep on biting and devouring each other,
Watch out or you will be destroyed by each other."
(Galatians 5:13-15)

"Love does no harm to its neighbor. Therefore love is
the fulfillment of the law." (Romans 13:10)
Abuse as described on a poster in an elementary
school:

> "Violence and/or disrespectful behavior is:
> any word, look, sign or act
> that hurts a person's body, possessions,
> dignity or security."

REFUGE

The shelter is open
Reach for the door
The cold will demolish
....frozen

Wind whirls around you
Screeching and bitter
It silences whispers
....secrets

You wrap yourself tightly
Shielding the tumult
The onslaught destroying
....beaten

It buffets and batters
Assaulting your nature
Stealing your person
....slaughter

Terror is ending
No more surrender
Degrading is over
....escape

Walk away slowly
Run away sure
Hasten for shelter
....done

A light in the distance
Beckons a loved one
Bask in the safety
....secure

God is your Lover
A-waiting embraces
He loves you, He saves you
....refuge

—Ellis February 2014

Section I
GOD CREATES

I believe God made the world.

I believe God made me.

I believe God has a plan for this world.

I believe God has a plan for me.

I believe God is Sovereign over all.

I. GOD CREATES

Day 1: God Made You

M y head is down. My spirit? Crushed. My emotions? Torn. My mind? Confused. I'm left alone,
defeated, trashed. I feel trapped, assaulted, degraded.
And I scream it, "Where is God for me?"

The door for your shelter has opened. You have suffered in silence, crying cold tears. But God is breaking
through to wrap you in His arms. Search for Him,
and find that He is your rescue. He can make beauty
from ashes, light in the darkness, and warmth in the
frigid air.

Your eyes have crusted over, but God is wiping your
tears. All that you dreamed for, all that you wanted, all
that you need is found in Him. Break away with me
and seek Him earnestly with all your heart.

It takes faith to see Him, faith to find Him, faith to
rest in His arms. Take that step with me.

"And without faith it is impossible to please God, because anyone who comes to him must believe that he exists and that he rewards those who earnestly seek him." (Hebrews 11:6)

That's the purpose of this devotional book—to earnestly seek God. Those who have lived with abuse in this world may feel a deep chasm between them and God. Where is He in all the turmoil? Well, God has been there from the beginning.

"In the beginning God create..." (Genesis 1:1)

Believing in the first verse of the Bible is the start of looking to God as the Sovereign Maker and Ruler of all. This verse says that God created it ALL. He has left his footprint over all the wonders of creation. But is He here for me in all my despair? Did he create us and then leave us? We need to believe in His words that that say He truly IS with us, every moment.

"...God has said, 'Never will I leave you;
never will I forsake you.'
So we say with confidence,
'The Lord is my helper;

I will not be afraid.
What can man do to me?"'
(Hebrews 13:5b-6)

If you have never stepped out to seek God, I ask you to give Him a chance. In the treachery and violence of domestic abuse, we can lose sight of the fact that God is there for us. But I challenge you to put your doubts aside, and take some time to listen for God to speak. Yes, it does take faith, but God gave us a promise. He will reward those who diligently seek Him.

Genesis chapters 1 and 2 tell the story of God's massive creation. The water, the air, the ground. The mountains, the oceans, the deserts. The stars, the sun, the moon. The fish of the sea and the birds of the air. The trees, the grass, the flowers. The fruit, the vegetables, and all growing grains. Animals of all kinds.

What a plan! Everything was made to sustain life in an unending cycle. The rain and sun, producing growth and sustenance. All of creation coming alive with water, rising up to the clouds and coming down in the rain. The seeds in abundance, to plant and replant and replant again. And in this creation the animals of the earth were all given their place.

And finally, the crown of His creation came as He created man from the dust of the earth. Amazingly, God created male and female "in His image":

> *"So God created man in his own image,*
> *in the image of God he created him;*
> *male and female he created them."*
> (Genesis 1:27)

That's a sobering thought. Created in the image of God. To me that means we have a very special place in all of His creation. In ways hard to understand, we are somehow a mirror of Him. And even more than being made in His image, He brought us into a special place of awareness as He *"breathed into his nostrils the breath of life, and the man became a living being"* (Genesis 2:7). It was truly a beautiful picture in that Garden.

God's final work was to create woman, from the rib of the man, close to his heart. He would care for her, she would care for him, and together they would *"fill the world and subdue it"* (Genesis 1:28).

> *"And God saw all that he had made, and it was*
> *very good."* (Genesis 1:31)

Do you feel like a special creation before God? YOU ARE! Human beings are given a soul and a spirit that doesn't exist in other parts of creation. We are set apart for God, truly something extraordinary. And in His creation of us, God would be able to show his great and unending love.

It was a perfect picture, until sin entered the world. Starting with the disobedience of Adam and Eve (Genesis 3), God knew in His ultimate wisdom that He would need to send a Savior, and He sent "his only begotten son" (John 3:16) Jesus into the world. And in this He would show his great love for us. Jesus came willingly, knowing that the end would mean dying on a cross for the sins of the world. But out of love for us, Jesus did come, He did die for our sins, and He did rise again.

Does this make you feel special in the eyes of God? Did he choose some people to die for, and not others? No, God looks at all of us the same. In fact, each one of us in His creation is an original:

"For you created my inmost being;
You knit me together in my mother's womb.
I praise you because I am fearfully
and wonderfully made;

Your works are wonderful, I know that full well.
My frame was not hidden from you.
When I was made in the secret place.
When I was woven together in the depths of the earth,
Your eyes saw my unformed body."
(Psalm 139:13-15)

Does that make you feel special in God's eyes? He formed you just as you are when still in your mother's womb. I want every one of you reading this to get a bigger image of how important you are in the eyes of God. In the midst of domestic abuse, God's loving care for us as a special creation can seem to get lost. Does God see what is happening here? Can He help me and rescue me out of the violence?

It is important to remember that from the very beginning of creation, the battle for right living is continually being attacked because of SIN. Abuse is sin! Hurting another is SIN. Dominating another is SIN. Degrading another is SIN. Violence is SIN. And sin is a spoiler of God's beautiful creation. God looks at us in the treachery, and He weeps. But He then gives us every victory to be overcomers when the assault of sin is hurled against us.

Listen to these words of how special you are to God. Listen to what God thinks of YOU. You don't have to listen to negative messages aimed at hurting you. Don't believe them! You are not stupid. You are not ignorant. You are not ugly. You are not crazy. Believe what God says about you: you are *"fearfully and wonderfully made"* (Psalm 139:14).

The glorious part of God's plan is that His Spirit was with us from the very beginning, as *"the Spirit of God was hovering over the waters"* (Genesis 1:1). He has not created us and then abandoned us. In fact, the opposite is true. As He walked in the garden with Adam and Eve (Genesis 3:8), He showed that He was personally there for them, and He is personally here for us as well. He created us to have a union with us, each one of us, all the time, in every situation, throughout our joys and throughout our sorrows.

When the hurts of life seem to defeat us, it is only too easy to become bitter and spiteful and retaliatory. We want to strike back and defend ourselves. Sometimes the hurts are so severe that we lose any strength we ever had in ourselves. We easily succumb and just "take it." But does God want us to shrivel and cower in a corner, afraid to move to the right or to the left? No, that is NOT His plan for us.

Remember! God made you, God loves you and God is with you! And God will lead you to a life of freedom in Christ.

> *"When you pass through the waters,*
> *I will be with you;*
> *And when you pass through the rivers,*
> *They will not sweep over you.*
> *When you walk through the fire,*
> *You will not be burned;*
> *The flames will not set you ablaze.*
> *For I am the LORD, your God . . ."*
> (Isaiah 43:2-3)

Take a step of faith and BELIEVE IT. God made you, God loves you, and you are precious in His sight. You have a future and a hope with Him.

> ***". . .Since you are precious and honored in***
> ***my sight, and because I love you."***
> (Isaiah 43:2-4).

I. GOD CREATES

Day 2: God Gifted You

There is nobody else on earth that is exactly like YOU. Your hair, your eyes, your voice, your fingerprints, your talents, your gifts, your purpose. God says clearly in His Word that each one of us is created differently. We each have qualities and talents that the Lord has given us to serve Him and to serve others. He has a unique place for every one of us. Where He uses you is a different place than where He uses me in His service. In the end, as our life ends, the most blessed words to hear are:

"Well done, good and faithful servant!
You have been faithful with a few things.
I will put you in charge of many things.
Come and share your master's happiness."
(Matthew 25:23)

In the ravages of abuse—physical, mental, emotional, or spiritual—it is possible that the victim can lose a perspective of who she really is and what her qualities are. Over and over again she is given negative messages in many ways from an abuser. It could start in her nuclear family, from her parents or siblings. Before she ever got married, her self-esteem was not clear in her mind. Finding a partner who seems strong and capable makes her feel more secure. The marriage proposal seems to come quickly after meeting each other, and she is only more than willing to say "Yes." Someone needs her, someone wants her.

But the early glow of marriage gradually erodes into a feeling of being stifled. He doesn't want her to go out with friends. In fact, he doesn't like any of her friends. He controls her money and her purchases. He wants her to stay home. Slowly the criticisms become more intense. He doesn't like the cooking. She doesn't clean the house well enough. When she brings up a subject for discussion, it only ends in argument. And then name-calling starts. The anger increases. He starts throwing things and pounding the walls. She is becoming more fearful of what might happen next. She doesn't dare talk to anyone. After all, when the couple is in the public arena, they look like the perfectly married husband and wife. He puts his arm around her, saying, "She is mine." And they may even go to church regularly.

But what has she lost? As an adult, she feels no freedom to go where she wants to go. Someone else is telling her how to spend her money. She would like to get a job, but he makes it very difficult. If she does make some money, he is in charge of how it is spent. She has hobbies to enjoy, but they all take time away from him. Frankly, she has been bound with chains—her every action controlled by him.

Is this why she is on this earth? To serve one man? Who is it that should guide her steps? Her husband? Where is God in this picture?

The truth is that this marriage is distorted and dysfunctional in the highest degree. She has lost freedom to be who she is, and he holds all the ropes. Is this God's design for marriage? Actually in a healthy marriage, the couple works together to face the challenges of life. They look to God's Word for guidance and for character building. They are "one in spirit" and share the same goals. Does one rule over the other? Never!

Both husband and wife look for ways to BLESS each other, not control each other. Blessing means encouraging each other to become all that God created you to be. In a healthy relationship, they may do many things together, but they also develop their own gifts and talents and seek out their personal goals in life.

God has blessed each of us with certain gifts in order that we can serve each other. It's like a large jigsaw puzzle in which every piece has a place. God's Word parallels this arrangement to all the parts in a human body. Every part has a purpose and no one has more importance than the other.

"The eye cannot say to the hand, 'I don't need you!'
And the head cannot say to the feet, 'I don't need you!'
On the contrary, those parts of the body that seem to
be weaker are indispensable, and the parts that we
think are less honorable we treat with special honor."
(I Corinthians 12:21-23)

If you are not sure of your gifts, find a mature believer who can lead you to understanding how God has gifted you. I Corinthians 12 – 14 will give good insight. Then thank God for HOW He has made you. Remember that He has gifted us so that we can serve others.

"Now to each one the manifestation of the Spirit is
given for the common good."
(I Corinthians 12:7)

"There are different kinds of gifts, but the same Spirit.
There are different kinds of service, but the same Lord.
There are different kinds of working
but the same God works all of them in all men."
(I Corinthians 12:4-6)

"All these are the work of one and the same Spirit
and he gives them to each one, just as he determines."
(I Corinthians 12:11)

Never forget that you are a precious creation of God. No one has the right to define who you are and what you can or cannot do. You won't flourish with criticism, with anger, with threats, with deprivation, with abandonment, with name-calling, with slaps, with "crazy-making." You flourish under God's divine love and protection and guidance. And NO PERSON has the right to take that away from you. Thank God for how He has created you and gifted you. Then use those gifts to serve Him and others.

"For we are God's workmanship,
created in Christ Jesus to do good works,
which God prepared in advance for us to do."
(Ephesians 2:9-10)

I. GOD CREATES
Day 3: God Is Glorified

This is a difficult subject to discuss but so important as we try to find meaning in this life. Glorifying God is the BIG picture we need to see. What does it mean for God to be "glorified"? And how do we glorify God?

God's Word says that we bring praise to God Almighty when we come into a relationship with Him. His purposes for us are to give us the very best life has to offer. He wants to give us the fullness of life, "abundant life."

> *"I have come that they may have life,*
> *and have it to the full."*
> (John 10:10)

Somehow in God's plan, He creates us, He loves us, He rescues us, He delivers us, and it all brings praise and glory back to Him. It's a love relationship at the deepest level. Almighty God loving us, and proving it by sending His only Son Jesus to die in our place for our sins. And the end is life eternal with Him.

"For God so loved the world
that He gave His one and only Son
that whoever believes in Him should not perish
but have eternal life."
(John 3:16)

Jesus did not come to condemn us, or leave us abandoned here on earth, but in fact to save us from damnation.

"For God did not send His Son into the world to
condemn the world, but that the world
through Him might be saved."
(John 3:17)

THAT'S what brings glory to God. US!

How does domestic abuse bring glory to God? The answer is simple. It cannot, and it never will. God's design for a marriage follows the same guidelines as our relationships with everyone else in the world. It should be marked by the kindness and goodness of Jesus Himself as His Spirit fills us.

"Love must be sincere.
Hate what is evil; cling to what is good.
Be devoted to one another in brotherly love.
Honor one another above yourselves.
Never be lacking in zeal,
but keep your spiritual fervor, serving the Lord."
(Romans 12:9-11)

For those caught in domestic abuse, the questions seem to overwhelm us. Why is he one person in public and another person behind closed doors? Why does he treat me like this? Doesn't he love me? Is this how marriage works? Did God forsake me? Did I do something "wrong" to deserve this?

The simple answer from Jesus Himself is that life on this earth is not without trials and troubles. In fact, He said we should EXPECT difficulties:

"I have told you these things,
so that in me you may have peace.
In this world you will have trouble.
But take heart! I have overcome the world."
(John 16:33)

Did Jesus live this life without trouble?

"He was despised and rejected by men,
a man of sorrows, and familiar with suffering.
Like one from whom men hide their faces
he was despised, and we esteemed him not."
(Isaiah 53:3)

So when He says He understands our sufferings, He means it. Domestic abuse makes me feel that way, "despised and rejected." But Jesus says that He can overcome the world, even in the midst of domestic abuse.

Somehow in God's great plan for us, it is our suffering that brings us closer to God Himself through the very presence of Jesus Christ in our lives with the indwelling of the Holy Spirit. For me, I don't know any place to find deliverance from the assaults of domestic abuse, outside of God and His Word.

This is why!

God calls abuse "sin." He gives us strength to see the truth and then to act on it. He has promised to be with us through our trials, and bring us out with a sense of peace. His love is forever. His peace is deeply felt. His hope gives us a future. Serving Him gives us a deep sense of purpose. His joy comes as we feel His hand working on our behalf. He puts a grateful and thankful spirit in our hearts that helps us rise above the turmoil, trusting Him for the outcome. And He says that these trials are only temporary as we look forward to eternity in His presence.

What else do we need?

I firmly believe that we are not to stay stuck in an abusive relationship. In fact, simply enduring assaults against us only enables someone else to sin and sin again. God tells us to confront sin. There are support systems out there, both in therapy and in the church. We need to surround ourselves with people who speak truth and who are wise in their counsel. It is a tough battle, especially in our hearts. But Jesus is the great Healer. God is glorified when we live in obedience to Him.

> *"Bring my sons from afar and my daughters*
> *from the ends of the earth*
> *everyone who is called by my name,*
> *whom I created **for my glory**,* (emphasis mine)
> *whom I formed and made."*
> (Isaiah 43:7)

> *"The wild animals honor me,*

the jackals and the owls,
because I provide water in the desert and streams in
the wasteland,
to give drink to my people, my chosen,
the people I formed for myself
*that they may **proclaim my praise.***
(Isaiah 43:20-21)

Take refuge in the fact that you are a big part of God's greater purposes. As we pull closer to Him, and He pulls closer to us, it brings all the glory to Almighty God as we relish in all He has done and all that He is. Proclaim His praise! Following Him in obedience— that's what brings glory to God.

"This is my Father's glory,
that you bear much fruit,
showing yourselves to be my disciples."
((John 15:8)

Footnote: To more fully understand the glory of God, read the book of John and look for the word "glory." Actually it is throughout the Scriptures.

I. GOD CREATES

Day 4: God Gave Marriage

It was God who instituted the covenant of marriage, not only as a way to propagate the species, but also for us to learn about love and life. Marriage is the great equalizer, bringing us out of ourselves. It is a major place for us to learn and grow and develop character.

The union of male and female is concurrent in all of creation—plants and animals. God desired for members of the human species to have a partnership—male and female as in all creation. *The LORD God said, 'It is not good for the man to be alone. I will make a helper suitable for him"* (Genesis 2:18). The "suitable helper" was not found in all the beasts of the field nor in all the birds of the air (Genesis 2:19). It took a woman to fulfill the role of suitable partner.

"Then the LORD God made a woman from
the rib he had taken out of the man,
and he brought her to the man.
The man said, 'This is now bone of my bones and flesh
of my flesh; she shall be called WOMAN, for she was
taken out of man."
(Genesis 2:22-23)

From the very beginning, the plan was for marriage to bring two imperfect people together who will be devoted to each other despite their imperfections. Are they perfect? Are they sinless? No. Our sinful nature showed up early with the first couple, Adam and Eve. They were given a free choice to obey God or not, and when they chose wrongly, their sinful natures were exposed (Genesis 3). From the beginning of time, humanity has had this sinful nature. We are no different than Adam and Eve. Jesus also showed us how to deal with our inevitable differences in marriage, giving grace and forgiveness to each other as He gives to us. That's how it's supposed to work.

The first step in the union of marriage is for the husband to shift his dedication from his parents to his wife.

"For this reason a man will leave his father and mother and be united to his wife, and they will become one flesh." (Genesis 3:24)

Sadly, when this command is disregarded, the marriage will never find fulfillment. Does he really "leave" his parents and "cleave" to his wife? Is she first? Or does the bond with the parents take first priority? In many abusive relationships, the husband has never really left his parents. The wife is secondary.

The second step is to realize that marriage is a place to tend to the needs of each other. Is he able to put the needs of his wife ahead of his own, or is he focused on meeting his own needs? Is she willing to respect her husband and to unselfishly tend to his needs as a "helpmate"?

"Each of you also must love his wife as he loves himself, and the wife must respect her husband." (Ephesians 5:33)

That's the plan!

This godly union is only possible if both husband and wife have the same purpose or mission in life. Are they one in their spirits? Paul makes a general

statement about the nature of a God-honoring relationship, and it applies first to the union of marriage.
He writes to the people of Philippi, saying,

> *"...then make my joy complete by being like-*
> *minded, have the same love, being **one in***
> ***spirit and purpose.*** (emphasis mine)

> *Do nothing out of selfish ambition or vain conceit,*
> *but in humility consider others better than yourselves.*
> *Each of you should look not only to your own interests,*
> *but also to the interests of others."*
> (Philippians 2:2-4)

Putting the needs of others ahead of your own is
the standard for success in all relationships, but especially within a marriage. First, in the newly created
union of a marriage, the wife is FIRST instead of the
parents. Second, they both leave selfishness behind,
"looking to the interest of others." Third, the union
should be complete—physically, emotionally, and
(most importantly) spiritually.

A couple can become "one flesh" without being
"one spirit." If the spiritual oneness in the relationship is absent, the union is eventually headed for

trouble. The longer their union is together, the more important their spiritual beliefs become. Spirituality burrows into the very core of our personhood. What do we believe to be true? What is our first priority in life? What is the purpose of our existence? Do we believe in God? Do we look to Jesus and the Word of God for guidance? Can we worship together, pray together, share Scriptures together? Sadly, many couples begin their lives together by being "unequally yoked" (2 Corinthians 6:14), or not the same in their spirits or their faith. They are not "one in spirit and purpose." Being unequal in the innermost core of your life promises to lead to difficulty. The "oneness" will have a huge gap.

It started with that first couple, Adam and Eve. Their sinful natures were exposed from the beginning. They clearly disobeyed God by eating the forbidden fruit of the Tree of the Knowledge of Good and Evil. Above that, they refused to take responsibility for their sin, but instead blamed each other (Genesis 3). The snake (Satan) was the liar, but Adam and Eve were beset with refusing to take responsibility for their own actions. They blamed someone else for their sin. Blame is nothing but a cover-up, and a detriment to

Day 4: God Gave Marriage

relationships. It doesn't make the sin go away in the eyes of God. He sees the truth!

How easy it is to stoop to blaming others, to lie, to hide, to being irresponsible—to SIN.

In all of life, following God's ways is the ONLY way to live a full and complete life, especially in marriage. Without both the husband and the wife joining together in obedience to God's Word, the marriage is destined to have difficulty. Does sin happen in our daily lives? Yes, it does. But Jesus taught us to face our sin (confess), ask forgiveness, and then turn away from those sins. "Go, and sin no more," Jesus said when speaking to the woman caught in adultery (John 8). Keep our consciences clear before God.

If we don't face sin early, when it first happens, the pattern can deepen until the division in the marriage can have severe outcomes. Some of the problems can become extreme, and the union will risk becoming broken.

With the fruit of the Spirit is in our lives, relationships WORK!

"But the fruit of the Spirit is love, joy, peace,
patience, kindness, goodness,
faithfulness, gentleness and self-control.

Against such things there is no law."
(Galatians 5:22)

Relationships with these qualities will never fail. It's not something we can stir up within ourselves. In fact, the way to live within these qualities is to have the Spirit of God indwelling us. God freely gives it to us as we seek HIM first. If both husband and wife are indwelt by the Holy Spirit, the way of peace in the home should be evident. It's called "living by the Spirit":

"Since we live by the Spirit,
let us keep in step with the Spirit.
Let us not become conceited,
provoking and envying each other."
(Galatians 5:25-26)

Notice that several things are mentioned here that will compromise "living by the Spirit." Becoming conceited, provoking each other, and envying each other. In conceit, the only person who is important is YOU. It's all about you, not the other person. Provoking another means you deliberately do or say things that upset the other person. And envy is one of the first signs of an unhealthy relationship. Envy and jealousy are self-centered characteristics, not a loving response to another person.

So God gives us ways to build relationships that are healthy and wholesome, and bring the glory to Him. His way? It works! Without Him? There is trouble.

"...look...to the interests of others."

(Philippians 2:4)

Day 5: God Made a Helpmate

God recognized from the very beginning that man needs a "helpmate."

> *"The LORD God said, 'It is not good for the man*
> *to be alone. I will make a*
> *helper suitable for him.*
> (Genesis 2:18)

A "helper" could be defined as someone who is "strong to help the weak." That would imply that the woman brings some strength to the relationship that the man needs. And in the converse, the man brings something strong to the relationship that the woman needs.

After the sinful disobedience in the garden by both the woman and the man (Genesis 3), the LORD God cursed them both. The curse of the woman was two-fold: increased pain in childbirth and that the man will "rule" over her:

> *"To the woman he said,*
> *'I will greatly increase your pains in childbearing;*
> *with pain you will give birth to children.*
> *Your desire will be for your husband,*
> *and he will rule over you.'"*
> (Genesis 3:16)

Take note also that the woman will feel the need to look to her husband, as her "desire" will be for him. She will feel the need to let him "rule" over her.

The man was given the role of providing for the family. It would not be an easy task, as the ground would be plagued with "thorns and thistles." His toil would be full of pain, and he would need to work hard "by the sweat of his brow."

> *"Cursed is the ground because of you;*
> *through painful toil you will eat of it*
> *all the days of your life.*
> *It will produce thorns and thistles for you,*
> *and you will eat the plants of the field.*

*By the sweat of your brow you will eat your food
until you return to the ground, since from it you were
taken; for dust you are and to dust you will return."*
(Genesis 3:17-19)

All this because Adam listened to his Eve, and Eve listened to the serpent (Satan)! Both were guilty of disobedience to God by eating from the tree when God commanded them, *"You must not eat of it"* (Genesis 3:17).

So they both sinned, and now they both need each other to function in a balanced way. They both have difficulties, but together they can give each other support through the joys and trials of life.

That is the picture of marriage. Each has a role. It is like two feet walking forward—left foot, right foot. There is no progress unless they move in sync together. Each one needs the other! It's a mutual submission:

"Submit to one another out of reverence for Christ."
(Ephesians 5:21)

This arrangement only works when Christ is in the middle. First, we submit to Christ, the Lord and Ruler of all. Then we submit to each other. In marriage no one is "more powerful" or "more important" than the other. Each is to respect and honor the other. For the wife to submit to her husband, it is totally because she seeks his leadership and protection. He, of course, would always be looking out for her welfare and will value her help. It is not that he has the right to push her around or disregard her views. And for the husband to provide leadership? It is totally out of love for her, not to power over her. And, in the converse, he should value her insight as a "helpmate."

The example of the wife submitting to her husband is parallel to the church submitting to Christ for leadership.

*"**Wives** (emphasis mine) submit to your husbands as*
to the Lord, for the husband is the head of the wife
as Christ is the head of the church, his body,
of which he is the Savior.
Now as the church submits to Christ,
so also wives should submit to their husbands
in everything."
(Ephesians 5:22-24)

Likewise, the love of a husband for his wife is compared to the love Christ has for the church. And Jesus Christ gave his life, nailed to a cross, to save the church.

"Husbands (emphasis mine), *love your wives,*
just as Christ loved the church and gave himself up for
her to make her holy,
cleansing her by the washing with water through
the words,
and to present her to himself as a radiant church,
without stain or wrinkle or any other blemish,
but holy and blameless.
In this same way, husbands ought to love their wives
as their own bodies.
He who loves his wife loves himself.
After all, no one ever hated his own body, but he feeds
and cares for it,
just as Christ does the church. . ."
(Ephesians 5:25-29)

Now THAT is a great place to be. My husband loves me as Christ loves the church. How does a husband's love parallel the love of Christ? Christ *"gave himself for her," "presents her as radiant," "without blemish* (sin)," and *"he feeds and cares for her as his own body."* How does a wife's love parallel the love of Christ? By putting the needs of others ahead of her own, respecting him, and giving support as a "helpmate" to her husband.

It is impossible to imagine that Christ would abuse his bride, the church—or ME! Jesus is the embodiment of pure love, and He proved it by dying for our sins on the cross. Am I safe submitting to Christ? Will he ever hurt me? The opposite is true. Jesus Christ showers me with "one blessing after another."

"From the fullness of his grace we have all received one blessing after another."
(John 1:16)

It is safe to say that Christ would only shower me with the very best as I look to him for leadership. Likewise, His Word says that I certainly should be safe with a husband who loves me as he loves himself. A husband's love is to be so strong that he "*loves his wife as his own body.*" His role is to "*feed and care for (her)*" just as he feeds and cares for his own body. She should feel safe with him and he should feel safe with her. Intentional hurt has no place in this relationship.

If a man does not love himself, he really doesn't understand "love" and it could lead to abusing others.

If he cannot love himself, he has no reason to love anyone else. He doesn't care for himself, nor does he know how to care for others. In fact, he can't do it! Christ, as the embodiment of Love, can fix these defects, as we earnestly seek Him.

Should the role of "helpmate" include allowing a man to have destructive and hurtful behavior, directed at you or anyone else? Of course, the answer again is "No." The most helpful thing an abused woman can do is to stand up to violent, hurtful behaviors. Refuse to allow these assaults. Expect a change. Insist on something different. If he joins you in wanting to find a healthy, God-fearing marriage relationship, then change WILL COME. Give him a chance to find the true road to life as God intended. It may take time, but God has promised to make us a "new creation" (2 Corinthians 5:17). That means Christ CAN change it!

If he refuses to seek a change, then your role is to protect yourself and find a "safe place" to live. In the end, he will have to stand before Christ as His judge.

"...love his wife as he loves himself,
...and the wife must respect her husband."
(Ephesians 5:33)

I. GOD CREATES
Day 6: God Sends Children

In God's ultimate order of this world, children are given as a blessing:

> *"Sons are a heritage from the LORD,*
> *Children a reward from him.*
> *Like arrows in the hands of a warrior*
> *Are sons born in one's youth.*
> *Blessed is the man*
> *Whose quiver is full of them."*
> (Psalm 127:3-5a)

Not only are children viewed as a blessing, but they are given for an even deeper reason. It is the desire of the LORD that his Word be taught to the children throughout the generations. In the Old Testament the priest Levi was given the responsibility to teach the Word of God to the people:

"My covenant was with (Levi), a covenant of life and
peace, and I gave them to him;
this called for reverence and he revered me
and stood in awe of my name.
True instruction was in his mouth and nothing false
was found on his lips.
He walked with me in peace and uprightness,
and turned many from sin.
For the lips of a priest ought to preserve knowledge,
and from his mouth men should seek instruction—
because he is the messenger of the LORD Almighty."
(Malachi 2:4-7)

As Levi was to instruct the people in the Word of God, we also are considered to be the "messenger(s) of the Lord":

"These commandments that I give you today are to be
upon your hearts.
Impress them on your children.
Talk about them when you sit at home and when you
walk along the road,

when you lie down and when you get up."
(Deuteronomy 6:6-8)

The broad picture of God's purposes is for us to spread the truth of his Word throughout the world, passing it on to our children from generation to generation. Teaching His Word should start at home, and then expand to the community and to the world. As Jesus said after his resurrection and before his ascension to heaven:

"Therefore go and make disciples of all nations,
baptizing them in the name of the Father and of the
Son and of the Holy Spirit.
And teaching them to obey
everything I have commanded you.
And surely I am with you always,
to the very end of the age."
(Matthew 28:19-20)

God says he is seeking those who will be his "ambassadors" (2 Corinthians 5:20). And our first responsibility as an ambassador is to teach our children. God is looking for "godly offspring" within a marriage:

"Has not the LORD made them one?
In flesh and spirit they are his.
And why one? Because he was seeking godly offspring.
So guard yourself in your spirit,
and do not break faith with the wife of your youth."
(Malachi 2:15)

It's a heavy responsibility to be an example to our children so they in turn will grow to love and obey God. Unfortunately, the patterns learned in a dysfunctional home will also be taught. Children pick up the anger, the explosions, the terror, and it can become evident in their lives as well because they have been immersed in it. It's all they know. Unless there is an intervention along the line, the abuse can be passed down in a cycle of repetitious pain.

Children repeat what they have lived, what they have seen, what they have heard. And the devastation of abuse, divorce, cruelty, deprivation, and abandonment may be repeated in their lives if not confronted. Psychological evaluations about abuse patterns have stated that abuse is LEARNED. What children see, they repeat.

"Generations come and generations go,
But the earth remains forever. . .

What has been will be again,
What has been done will be done again;
There is nothing new under the sun."
(Ecclesiastes 1:4, 9)

This is why it is ultimately important for the cycle of abuse to be stopped in a family structure. The patterns will be repeated unless they are confronted. This should be one of the main reasons that abused wives need to find a way to stand up to abusive behaviors. But she must, for the safety of her children. Generations of abusive behaviors may be very difficult to break. Even though it is a very difficult journey, it is a deeply loving thing to do. It takes courage to take a stand and make some changes in the family dynamics as it is brought out in the open. Children CAN learn new ways of thinking and acting.

"You, my brothers, were called to be free.
But do not use your freedom to indulge the sinful
nature; rather, serve one another in love.
The entire law is summed up in a single command:
'Love your neighbor as yourself.'

If you keep on biting and devouring each other,

watch out or you will be destroyed by each other.
So I say, live by the Spirit, and you will not gratify the
desires of the sinful nature.
For the sinful nature desires what is contrary to the
Spirit, and the Spirit what is contrary
to the sinful nature."
(Galatians 5:13-17)

The risk of passing abusive behaviors to the children in the family is great. They see it, they experience it, and they will learn it. For the sake of breaking the chain of abuse that could last for generations, take that step away from it. This should be a strong incentive to bring the destructive relationships in the family to a halt. Your children need to see that you will NOT tolerate being assaulted—verbally, emotionally, physically. Be strong for them!

"...serve one another in love."
(Galatians 5:13)

I. GOD CREATES
Day 7: God's Family

I t is God's design that believers meet together frequently to give each other encouragement and support. He called us a "family."

> *"Let us consider how we may spur one another on*
> *toward love and good deeds.*
> *Let us not give up meeting together, as some are in*
> *the habit of doing, but let us encourage one another—*
> *and all the more as you see the Day approaching."*
> (Hebrews 10:24-25)

In simple terms, we NEED each other! We can easily get sidetracked and away from the truth. The Lord knew it would be healthy and helpful for us to meet together *"perfectly united in mind and thought"* (I Corinthians 1:10) so that we will be *"strong to the end."*

Ponder the thought that God calls us his "children" and He, Almighty God, is our Father! It puts us together in a family. His family!

"Yet to all who received him,
to those who believed in his name,
*he gave the right to become **children of God**—*
(emphasis mine)
children born not of natural descent, nor of human
decision nor a husband's will,
but born of God."
(John 1:12)

In another place, the Scriptures say in a different way that we are adopted into God's family:

*"In love he predestined us to be **adopted***
(emphasis mine)
as his sons through Jesus Christ,
in accordance with his pleasure and will—to the
praise of his glorious grace,
which he has freely given us in the One he loves."
(Ephesians 1:5-6)

Being part of God's family means that I have many brothers and sisters in Christ. And with God as my Father, I am fully protected and cared for in His forever family. That's right! This family never ends.

Being part of God's family also means that we watch out for each other.

"Live in peace with each other.
And we urge you, brothers, warn those who are idle,
encourage the timid,
help the weak, be patient with everyone.
Make sure that nobody pays back wrong for wrong,
but always try to be kind to each other and to
everyone else.
Be joyful always, pray continually;
give thanks in all circumstances,
for this is God's will for you in Christ Jesus."
(I Thessalonians 5:13-18)

Clearly these words are speaking to the group, the whole family, the whole church. It's a beautiful picture of how a family should look in the Light of Jesus Christ.

It is also in this family that we seek counsel in times of need. In our search for wisdom that comes from God, it is wise to turn to our mature brothers and sisters in Christ.

> *"Carry each other's burdens,*
> *and in this way you will fulfill the law of Christ."*
> (Galatians 6:2)

While in the turmoil of domestic abuse, it may not be easy to open up to others in the church. Not everyone will understand. Some may speak premature judgments, blaming one or the other. Others may come up with simple solutions, or quote Scripture with finality. Please understand that many people are not versed in the dynamics of domestic abuse. They can't possibly believe that something like this would happen to church members, but it does. Most people don't know what to say, or how to deal with it in the church. I have had people in the church say to me directly, "I just don't understand domestic abuse." Why is that? They haven't experienced it, and it is a well-kept secret.

Couples in domestic abuse don't need quick judgments from church members. They don't need people "taking sides" in the matter. What both the abuser and the victim need is LOVE and support from the church.

It takes trained professionals with domestic abuse experience to indulge in therapeutic counseling. There are other ways to be of help:

"Therefore, as God's chosen people, holy and dearly loved, clothe yourselves with compassion, kindness, humility, gentleness and patience.

"Bear with each other and forgive whatever grievances you may have against one another.
Forgive as the Lord forgave you.
And over all these virtues put on love, which binds them all together in perfect unity.
Let the peace of Christ rule in your hearts, since as members of one body you were called to peace. And be thankful."
(Colossians 3:12-15)

That's how we treat each other!

When a marriage becomes troubled, it usually is kept secret for a long time. Slowly it may come out when others see some problems developing. I remember the first time I uttered softly in a Bible study group, "My husband and I are having problems." I'll never forget their shocked faces. No one could believe it. Aren't we in church every Sunday? Now I know that my shocking secret is probably apparent in many churches. It's the "big secret." Why do I know it's there? Because I was one of those people, sitting in church, with my husband's arm around my shoulders. But when we went home, the picture totally changed.

Although the "secret" needs to come out before matters deteriorate, I caution victims to be very careful WHOM you open up to. It should be someone who is mature in Christ, knowledgeable in His Word, and compassionate about the approach. Why can this be a very dangerous step for the victim? Because at the core of domestic abuse is ANGER and RAGE. A careless word or phrase could trigger an explosion of wrath when behind closed doors. It is not something to be taken lightly. The abuser's greatest wrath may come when he is finally exposed in the light of the truth. When that day came for me, I was forced to get a restraining order from the courts to feel safe.

I had some horrific experiences in the church when I finally opened up to the wrong people. Someone told me I could not serve in the church anymore, and that I needed to sit in the back row with my restraining order. It was a very confusing time for me. In my aloneness, I couldn't stay at that church any longer.

Finally I found a compassionate pastor, schooled in domestic abuse, who had wise counsel and support. I was not judged. Rather I felt supported, and I paid attention to his words of guidance. He was wise enough to know his limits, and encouraged professional therapy. I knew I was in his prayers, and he checked in with me often.

When domestic abuse controls a marriage, it takes schooled counselors to deal with the issues. The couple needs professional counseling, hopefully bathed in God's Word. The role of the church is best served as the members are committed to praying for the couple and to sharing an encouraging word of Scripture.

"Let the word of Christ dwell in you richly as you teach
and admonish one another with all wisdom,
and as you sing psalms, hymns and spiritual songs
with gratitude in your hearts to God.

And whatever you do, whether in word or deed,
do it all in the name of the Lord Jesus,
giving thanks to God the Father through him."
(Colossians 3:16-17)

The church family should be there to pray for you and to build your faith in God as you seek Him. In your personal walk with God, stay close to the Lord daily! Read the Scripture, pray, and stay in a state of closeness to Him. But also find a group of devoted Christians who will stand by you, especially when times become difficult. You can support each other with scripture and prayer.

"...and over all these virtues put on love..."
(Colossians 3:14)

I. GOD CREATES
Day 8: Life to the Fullest

Do you think this applies to you? Is it God's design to give YOU a life that's filled to the fullest? Or does that privilege only belong to other people?

You see the big homes with a three-car garage and a boat parked on the lake, while you go home to a three-room apartment. You see the cosmetic counter at a department store and could never visualize your-self looking pretty, even with make-up. You drive your 10-year-old car and hope it keeps running, while you find a parking space next to a Ferrari. You are happy to find a sweater that fits at the thrift store, never thinking that you could someday buy something new at a department store. You save your coupons to go to a pizza place, while others are dining out on steak and wine. You know people who have been on numerous cruises and are still planning another one, when you barely have enough cash to get away for a weekend. You see apparent romance in the movies, and wonder if it is really possible.

Is that your picture of "life to the fullest"? Maybe God has another completely different idea for you. There are several principles to consider when looking at the purpose and goals for your life. His biggest blessings may come from INSIDE rather than from what is seen on the OUTSIDE.

First, God knows you (surely better than you know yourself). He knows what really will truly make you happy. We may look at others with envy, but that never makes things better. In fact, it could be true that you would be miserable trading places with someone else in life. Our trust in God rests in the fact that HE IS IN CONTROL. Pulling next to his omniscient (or all-knowing) plans for you is the BEST place to be.

Secondly, God made a promise that he will bless you with abundant life:

> *"I have come that they may have life,*
> *and have it to the full."*
> (John 10:10b)

In that same verse, Jesus says,

*"The thief comes only to steal and kill and
destroy."*

Who is this "thief?" Who is it that wants to take
and destroy anything and everything in your life? His
name is Satan.

"Be self-controlled and alert.
Your enemy the devil prowls around like a roaring lion
looking for someone to devour.
Resist him, standing firm in the faith. . ."
(I Peter 5:8-9)

Satan is the "Father of lies" (John 8:44) and wants
to lead you away into pursuits that will bring no fulfillment in the end. Placing our goals into acquiring
wealth to acquire more and more stuff is a short-
sighted goal.

"Whoever loves money never has money enough;
whoever loves wealth is never satisfied with his
income. This too is meaningless."
(Ecclesiastes 5:10)

There must be MORE to life than this.

But Satan tempts and lures us into the wrong priorities.

"For everything in the world—the cravings of sinful man, the lust of his eyes and the boasting of what he has and does—comes not from the Father but from the world."

(I John 2:16)

- "Cravings." Longing for material possessions, money, joy rides.
- "Lust." Seeking to satisfy sexual desires, and other appetites.
- "Boasting." Looking for fame and fortune, high positions, praise of men.

All of these goals end in nothing. This life is focused on pleasing self, not others, or God. In the end, all turns to dust.

"From dust you came, and to dust will you return."

(Ecclesiastes 3:20)

In coming to God by faith, we learn that his priorities for our lives are the only priorities that matter. He says, in fact, to seek HIM first:

"For the pagans run after all these things,
and your heavenly Father knows that you need them.
But seek first his kingdom and his righteousness,
and all these things will be given to you as well."
(Matthew 6:32-33)

The conclusion is that God knows what we REALLY need. He knows the source of happiness, deep inside. He gives us things that are intangible: love, joy, peace. He gives us relationships that are real and supportive. He gives us comfort in his Word. He gives us purpose and a reason for living. He gives us endless promises about being with us, every moment of every day. He overcomes our greatest enemy, death, by giving us resurrection in Christ and eternal life.

So in our priorities, are we living for God or living for the things of the world?

"Do not store up for yourselves treasures on earth,
where moth and rust destroy,
and where thieves break in and steal.

But store up for yourselves treasures in heaven,
where moth and rust do not destroy, and where
thieves do not break in and steal. For where your trea-
sure is, there your heart will be also."
(Matthew 6:19-21)

Victims of domestic abuse sometimes feel that everything is lost. Life has taken a confusing dive. Expectations have been dashed. Trust is broken. Uncertainty is overwhelming. What we thought would end in happiness, has only turned into despair. But if we earnestly make an intentional effort to seek God, He will answer us and begin life anew. He is there for us in our deepest distress. He will be there for us as we rebuild and restore our lives to sanity. Will it be different? Yes. Will it be better? YES!

If both the husband and the wife feel the need to make changes, and commit to working on the relationship, then healing can come as you seek God's principles. Reconciliation is possible, and the restoration of a healthy marriage is within reach. Commit to being accountable to wise counselors, and expect God to work.

But if you are walking alone, either temporarily or permanently, your life is not over. You found the courage to walk away from a destructive relationship and healing is in process. It takes time as you work on new principles day by day. Patiently wait for God to build a new life for you. Pray for healing of your mind and your spirit. Repress any evil or vindictive thoughts that may come to your mind. You don't need to go there anymore. Your abuser is God's problem, not yours.

Old things have to be let go. Holidays are different, your workday may be different, your finances may be different, your lodging may be different. But the old is not a good place. You are done with it. Let God create a whole new life in you!

"But seek first his kingdom and his righteousness,..."
(Matthew 6:33).

I. GOD CREATES

Prayer of God's Creation

Father God, our Creator,
You are the Author of life
And the Creator of all that lives and breathes.
In Your creative mind, every individual is made
differently.
We are made unique and gifted by You
And You can use us all in different ways.
In Your creative mind, You have a plan for life
on earth.
And You have a plan for me!
I praise You that I am wonderfully made!
In Christ, You have revealed Your strong love for us.
You created us, and then reached out in divine love
for us.
The future is bright as You walk with me here,
Day by day.
And You have promised life with You into eternity,
One that begins now and never ends.
I need a fresh start with You, Lord.
Show me the way.

Now, Lord, *"create in me a clean heart, O God,*
And renew a right spirit within me." (Psalm 51:10)
Use me, Lord, for Your honor and glory.
Amen

Section II

God Loves

II. GOD LOVES
Day 9: Pearl of Great Price

Abused women don't feel loved. Period. Exclamation point! They not only feel unloved, but forsaken, abandoned, crushed, and defeated. Not only by their abuser, but also by many others, and sometimes they even feel forsaken by God.

Proverbs says that the "*earth trembles*" and "*cannot bear up*" over "*an unloved woman who is married...*"(Proverbs 30:23). When I first saw this verse, I felt, "that's me."

After years of abuse and neglect, this is how many victims can feel. She hears songs about love and watches movies about romance. It all seems so beautiful. But why is she deprived of this lovemaking? She gets sex, but is it about love?

Derogatory treatment assaults our personality so that we may lose any feelings about who we are. There are so many negative messages directed at our personhood, and after awhile a victim may start to believe them. Her inner core has been attacked and her belief system is shattered. What she thought would work in her marriage, doesn't work.

Maybe she is "unloved."

How is it that an abuser can find a victim, and a victim can end up with an abuser? When they first met, she looked at him as strong and confident. He would fill her deep feelings of inadequacy. He comes on strong, and makes her feel that he NEEDS her, all the time. And on the other hand, he thinks that he can "rescue" her, and that makes him feel important. She follows him around like a puppy dog, and he thinks he can do whatever he wants. He actually never asks her opinion, on anything.

Many abuse victims will say that their husband "swept them off their feet" and marriage came quickly. But once married, the faucet of love and care seemed to be turned off, or maybe just trickled with a few drops here and there. She wonders, "Where is love?" Slowly her smile starts to fade, and she feels trapped in a marriage that just doesn't feel right. Something is missing. Everything she does or says is questioned.

Her opinions are refuted or completely ignored. He makes all the decisions.

The truth is that both an abuser as well as a victim have a weak core in their personalities. They are not sure who they are—what they like, what they don't like. They are thrilled to maybe find some "completeness" with another person, so they jump at the chance. That other person is meeting her needs, and she is meeting his needs. But the "soul mate" union doesn't seem to develop. It's all surface.

Before long the newness of marriage wears off, and false fronts start to erode. The frustrations of life start to mount, and the couple isn't equipped to face them with maturity and responsibility. They don't communicate well. They never have learned much about the skills needed to have an authentic relationship.

The marriage got off to the wrong start, and now is deteriorating. They don't seem to know how to satisfactorily solve the problems that come in life. He starts to use force to silence her and get his way. At first she succumbs to his unusually aggressive behavior. Then the fear starts to build. Surely it's just a "phase" and will get better. Will it? Her fear slowly begins to deepen as his aggression increases.

The problem is that the couple got married for the wrong reasons. You can NEVER find fulfillment in another person. We are just not capable of doing this for each other. The marriage relationship should come together because both are living for the same purpose, and they partner and move together toward that goal in life.

"...make my joy complete by being like-minded, having the same love, being one in spirit and purpose. Do nothing out of selfish ambition or vain conceit..."
(Philippians 2:2-3)

This is such a core principle for a healthy marriage. *"NOTHING out of selfish ambition."* It's obvious to say that human love will never compare to God's love. We are imperfect beings. Marriage is a bit of a picture of what love should and could be, but it never perfectly gets there. Still, we should be able to find a commonality in life with a partner so that both the husband and wife can move forward in a positive and productive way. They give each other respect and support as they pursue the same goals in life. It's all about both being committed to doing things God's way!

Abuse ridden relationships can't and don't do this. One person dominates and smothers another. The behavior in the relationship becomes part of a downward spiral. She feels degraded and confused. His anger keeps her there. It seems like everything becomes a "game" or a power struggle.

But God's love is different. We are made in His image and His love is unending. Nobody is "junk!" Nobody deserves to be beaten up and degraded, ignored and abandoned.

Jesus gives us a beautiful picture of how precious we are to God with this story of The Pearl:

"Again, the kingdom of heaven is like a merchant looking for fine pearls.
When he found one of great value, he went away and sold everything he had and bought it."
(Matthew 13:45-46)

Again in this passage, Jesus tells the story of the Hidden Treasure:

"The kingdom of heaven is like
a treasure hidden in a field.
When a man found it, he hid it again,

> *and then in his joy went*
> *and sold all he had and bought that field."*
> (Matthew 13:44)

Now imagine that you are that tiny pearl "of great value" and you are lost in a field. God will search until he finds you. Or maybe he hides that one pearl in a field to protect you, and then joyfully rescues you again by selling all he has and buying that whole field just to have you.

I love this analogy. Me. I'm that one "pearl of great value." He would "sell everything he had" to purchase me. Then he hides this treasure (me) in a field, or protects me. He knows where I am, and He can find me, a pearl, in a field. It's like I am in the mud, but God sees and knows where I am. And he joyfully rescues me. He took control of the whole field so that he could hold me again. This is a picture of how much God loves you and me.

I wear lots of pearls in my jewelry, just to remind me of how precious I am to God.

That's right! We are of great value to God. He sent His son Jesus to show us the path to life. He IS LOVE for every person on earth, and the abuse makes him weep. It's not part of his design for anyone.

Think of yourself as that Pearl of Great Price! You ARE that Pearl—shining, beautiful, precious, and hidden safely in God. He CAN bring your smile and your peace back again and He will! Never forget how valuable you are to God.

"He...sold everything he had and bought it..."
(Matthew 13:46).

II. GOD LOVES

Day 10: Engraved on His Palms

G od knows everything about us. We are not born on this earth and then forgotten. In fact, God knows every detail about us, from our deepest thoughts to the very number of hairs on our head. He made us, He knows us, He cares about us.

"O LORD, you have searched me
And you know me.
You know when I sit and when I rise;
You perceive my thoughts from afar.
You discern my going out and my lying down;
You are familiar with all my ways.
Before a word is on my tongue
You know it completely, O LORD."
(Psalm 139:1-4)

"For you created my inmost being;
You knit me together in my mother's womb."
(Psalm 139:13)

It is comforting to know that God is PRESENT in our lives from the very beginning of life, even before we are born. By faith we can see His mighty hand at work throughout our lives.

Another picture He gives is one of being "engraved" on the palms of His hands, and that feels strong and secure. Can you picture a tattoo, or an engraving that will always be there?

"I will not forget you! See, I have engraved you
on the palms of my hands. . ."
(Isaiah 49:15b-16)

That's PERMANENT!

Open your hand and visualize your name written on your palm. Now slowly close your fingers tight over your name. That is where you are in God's hands. You are grasped tightly, never to be forgotten, never to be lost, never to be abandoned. If you don't have enough faith at this moment to believe you are secure in God's hands, pray about it, asking God to increase your faith.

Look for God throughout your day from the beginning to the end. View God's created world—the trees, the flowers, the grass, the blue sky, the clouds, the sun, the gentle breeze. All of it reminds us of God's touch on creation, a picture of His presence. Start the day thanking Him for his beautiful creation. Ask Him to use you for His purposes during the day. And as you crawl into bed at night, praise Him for being with you all day and all night. This can be called "practicing the presence" of God Almighty in our every moment.

After being abandoned by an abusive husband (either emotionally or physically), a victim may feel that God has abandoned her too. I know women who live in the same house with an abusive husband, and they never feel able to talk. I know other husbands who pull the disappearing act by refusing to communicate. Both are called "abandonment." My husband used to leave the house in the midst of a "discussion" and drive away in the car. I thought I had said something to upset him, and dropped the subject.

Never forget that God is grieved with this sin. He weeps over the devastation that comes with sin. Can you imagine Jesus never looking at you, never talking to you, and forgetting about you like you don't even matter? These could be called "sins of omission," or

NOT doing the right thing when you clearly know what you should be doing. But God has a rescue for us. He shows us clearly that this negligent behavior does not come from Him. It is sin from start to finish. Treating another like they are invisible, or not even there, is a sin. It is not of God.

So how do we stay close to God in this turmoil and confusion?

First, we need to acknowledge to ourselves that these passive aggressive acts against us have no truth in them. Remember that God created you and He loves you as you are. There is nothing that you did or did not do to "deserve" this punishment. The abuser is trying to make you crawl back to him, doing what he wants you to do. Of course, the "silent treatment" is not the way to solve anything. Remember that He holds us firmly in His hand—engraved, never to be lost. He is there, and he offers us His protection.

Second, He has put His divine Word into our hands. We can learn the Lord's ways by studying and meditating on the Scriptures when we are alone, or studying with others in a group. By reading His Word, we can remind ourselves again that He is there for us.

Third, we can pray by pouring out our griefs before Him. An abuse filled environment is surely not His will, so we need to get His guidance to learn how to handle it in His wisdom. We don't make impulsive decisions. In fact, it is vitally important that we receive some counsel from those in the church with knowledge of abuse as well as professional experts before making any major decisions. Covering every moment with prayer is a necessity.

Let Jesus be the reason you wake up every day, let Him lead you through your every moment, and let Him be the one who guides you. He WILL be there for you. Look for Him!

"I will praise you, O LORD, with all my heart;
I will bow down toward your holy temple
And will praise your name
For your love and your faithfulness,
For you have exalted above all things
Your name and your word.
When I called, you answered me;
You made me bold and stouthearted.

May all the kings of the earth praise you, O Lord,
when they hear the words of your mouth.
May they sing of the ways of the LORD,
For the glory of the LORD is great.

Though the LORD is on high,
He looks upon the lowly,
But the proud he knows from afar.
Though I walk in the midst of trouble,
You preserve my life;
You stretch out your hands
Against the anger of my foes,
With your right hand you save me.

The LORD will fulfill his purpose for me;
Your love, O LORD, endures forever—
Do not abandon the works of your hands."
(Psalm 138)

Day 11: God, Our Redeemer

We believe that God is our Designer, and God is our Lover, but he is also our Redeemer saving us with real protection and provision.

It is so easy for a woman in an abusive environment to believe that she is unable to take care of herself. Somehow she is convinced that she NEEDS her partner to take care of her, even with the abuse. She has a dependency on him, and she can't visualize being away from him. He actually makes her THINK she needs him, and that she would be lost without him. He may even utter those words out loud. She may hear threats that put fear in her heart if she makes any move on her own. What is a "threat"? "This or that" may happen if she does "this or that." Threats can also be characterized like this: "Do what I tell you or you are DEAD." It makes her feel trapped. It keeps her by his side, despite the maltreatment.

A common threat is for the abuser to say he will leave her, and she will "never see him again." Threatening divorce is ABUSE.

Jesus, however, told us not to be filled with fear about the affairs in our lives. Living with fear is not His design for us. Fear can be instilled over where to live, how to get food, how to find a job, etc. But Jesus says, "Do not worry," because He will always be there for us. Does she need an abusive husband to take care of her basic needs, or is Jesus enough?

"Do not worry about your life,
what you will eat or drink; or about your body, what
you will wear.
Is not life more important than food,
and the body more important than clothes?

Look at the birds of the air;
they do not sow or reap or store away in barns,
and yet your heavenly Father feeds them.
Are you not much more valuable than they?"
(Matthew 6:25-26)

I think maybe this verse is an answer to many of our fears. And Jesus confirms how valuable we really are to Him. "DO NOT WORRY" is actually a command.

It is so easy for a wife to conclude that she will be cared for in a marriage. It should be a partnership in which both the husband and the wife look out for the welfare of each other. That partnership assumes that both work together for a roof over their heads, some food in the kitchen, some clothes in the closet, and a job (or jobs) that can support these basic needs in life. We want to trust our partner. Assuming both will work together for basic needs is a fair assumption. But sometimes, an abuser will make an attempt to withhold these basic needs, just to get control and dependency upon his victim.

Jesus said to trust HIM. One of the strongest conflicts in the domestic abuse scenario is that the wife is fearful of leaving for a variety of reasons. Where will she go? Does she have money to survive? Can she find a job for support? Will they have to divide everything up? Will he still try to hurt her after she's gone?

The truth is that she will never, not ever, be alone, tossed out in the garbage like the trash. Not with God! He is our ultimate Redeemer. The meaning of that word comes from the Old Testament. If a woman loses her husband, the "redeemer" (or a next of kin) would marry her, providing her with protection and love. God says it directly as He calls himself a HUSBAND. A husband without failings. A husband full of promises. A husband that will never hurt. A husband that will always provide and protect.

It takes faith to be able to stand alone knowing that God, in the presence of the Holy Spirit, is with us always. Without Him, emotions of helplessness can overrun our thinking and make us feel weak.

If an abuser refuses to make some changes, and chooses to stay with his hurtful ways, it is best to just stay out of his way. You don't need to be the object of his wrath. In fact, it is a measure of strength to decide that you will not be beaten up another day in your life. Many women stay in an abusive relationship simply because they have no idea how they could take care of themselves without him. Don't let fear paralyze you.

Some women feel shame, or embarrassment over a failed marriage. Others think it is a complete disgrace, especially in the church. Other emotions that overwhelm us are a deep sense of sorrow or grief. Do you ask, "What will people think of us?" (shame). "Am I a complete failure?" (disgrace). "Why do I feel so sad all the time?" (sorrow). "I can't bear this loss" (grief).

God has an answer for you. Look how he overcomes these debilitating emotions:

*"**Fear not**; you will no longer live in **shame**.*
(emphasis mine)
*Don't be afraid; there is no more **disgrace** for you.*
You will no longer remember the shame of your youth
*and the **sorrows** of widowhood.*
For your Creator will be your husband;
the LORD of Heaven's Armies is his name.
He is your REDEEMER...
*For the Lord has called you back from your **grief**.*"
(Isaiah 54:4-6)

That's right. "FEAR NOT!" He is there as your Redeemer, to rescue you and get you out!

When we make a willful decision to turn our lives totally over to God, He gives us a complete make-over, making all things new. The old has gone. The new has come. We no longer have to wallow in the mud of abuse. It is a new and different life, to remove ourselves from the abusive environment, but things will only get BETTER with time. It's not easy to take a stand against sin. But just remember that the abusive nature is like a downward spiral, as it just gets worse. Don't let that happen!

"Therefore if anyone is in Christ, he is a new creation; the old has gone, the new has come."
(2 Corinthians 5:17)

In the Bible when Job lost everything—his family, his children, his possessions, his health—God restored him so that in the end Job had *"twice as much as he had before"* (Job 42:10).

"The LORD blessed the latter part of Job's life more than the first."
(Job 42:12).

The Lord may have some exciting things ahead for you also.

God can be the Redeemer that restores your marriage, but only as both parties seek Him. God can also be your Redeemer if you are walking alone. Trust God to lead you as you turn away from abuse. God, your Redeemer will never fail you.

***"Fear not; you will no longer live in shame.
Don't be afraid."***

(Isaiah 54:4)

II. GOD LOVES
Day 12: Names to Trust

Trust is the one thing that disappears in a dysfunctional family. You never know what is going to happen next. There is no way to predict it. This uncertainty keeps you walking on eggshells, waiting for the next "break."

Each day can seem to be full of "surprises." There's a swing between the "good" and the "bad" parts of the day. How long will the "good" last? How long will the "bad" last? If "trust" means being absolutely sure about someone, the mood swings in abuse can totally destroy it. As much as you WANT to trust, you can't completely embrace it. Things feel too uncertain.

(Domestic abuse counselors say that if you even FEEL afraid of something in your relationship, you should listen to those feelings and seek some professional guidance.)

In the domestic abuse cycle, there is a pattern that repeats and repeats and repeats again. There is a period of relative peace. Then something pops up that stirs emotions. Words were said or not said. Actions were questioned or criticized. Something was done or not done. Whatever it is, there comes an angry explosion from the abuser. He rants and raves, and tries to back her down. She may first try to defend herself, or she may just excuse herself to another room. If the tempers rise, she may try to leave the house. Then, almost as if there is a switch, he will suddenly change with a "sorry." He may do something special for her, like pick up flowers or take her to dinner. But the problem is that NO RESOLUTION was gained from the interaction. It is just forgotten, swept under the rug. She may blame herself, and just keep silent. Peace has returned for a while, until the cycle starts all over again.

Peace, then an issue, then an angry explosion, then a "sorry," then peace returns.

What can stop this angry cycle? The episodes seem to get more frequent and more violent as time goes by.

If this scene is in your life, if you feel more and more afraid, if the threats are becoming more than physical, then it is time to seek some support. These traumas usually don't fix themselves. There are deep reasons for accelerated anger and more explosive threats of assault. Good communication skills are obviously lost. Learning how to deal with differences, especially those that incite outbursts of anger, need to be learned. It is called "anger management." Skills can be learned if there is a sincere desire to make a change. Before things worsen to the extreme, it's time to face the fact that this union is not built on a rock but on slippery sand. It will wash away in the storm, unless there is a rescue.

Jesus told the story in Matthew chapter 7 of the house that was built on the sand (without Him) and the house that was built on the Rock (trusting Him). When the troubles come (wind, rain and floods), only those lives with faith in Jesus can stand firm and secure. Why is that? Trust! Jesus NEVER fails! He is the ROCK! And He is there!

Many people leave God to that one hour on Sunday morning, or maybe not even that. It's like signing in, and then signing out. When you step out of the quiet sanctuary, God is left behind. But God wants to be there for us day by day, moment by moment. He sees our in-comings and our out-goings. He doesn't force Himself on us, buts waits patiently for us to pull along-side Him.

Sometimes it takes times of deep distress to finally and humbly reach out to God. When a person comes to God, they learn that He relates to us in many ways. He is not a "One Hour Sunday Morning God." He is much more than that. Just look at His names. He has many names that describe who He is and how He relates to us.

- "Father" (Matthew 6:9)—providing and protecting
- "Shepherd" (John 10:14)—caring for his sheep (us)
- "King" (Psalm 44:4)—ruling with benevolence
- "Advocate" (Romans 8:34)—interceding for us
- "Counselor" (John 14:16)—giving us wisdom and guidance
- "Judge" (Psalm 7:11)—ruling in fairness and righteousness

The one I like the best in times of trouble is "The Rock" from the Matthew 7 story. I know what it feels like to feel planted on the sand, being tossed to and fro. If I am planted on the Rock (Jesus), then I am secure even through momentary trials.

In sign language the word "trust" is pictured with both hands invisibly holding tightly onto a rope overhead. Visualize hanging on for dear life to that rope, and then look up to see that God is holding onto the other end. And He will never let go. That is what trust is! I can trust the Rock!

The Scriptures are full of admonitions for us to trust God. When you trust God, you commit yourself and your future into His care. And you believe He will not fail you.

With the Psalmist below, do you also feel forgotten? Do you have sorrow in your heart? Do you feel your enemy triumphs over you? Take those thoughts and move them over to trusting in God's unfailing love.

"How long, O LORD? Will you forget me Forever?
How long will you hide your face from me?
How long must I wrestle with my thoughts
And every day have sorrow in my heart?
How long will my enemy triumph over me?

But I trust in your unfailing love;
My heart rejoices in your salvation.
I will sing to the LORD,
For he has been good to me."
(Psalm 13)

Being trapped in the cycle of abuse needs to stop. It is a very dangerous place to be. Who knows how the anger will end. If you are becoming aware that your relationship has deteriorated to the cycle of abuse, I beg you to seek out some help. Pray about your next step, and trust God to show you. My suggestion would be to find a domestic abuse advocacy group where you can discuss your situation with experienced counselors. They will know how to protect you as you move forward to taking the next step. You MUST have people surrounding you, and hopefully those people make prayer part of their assistance.

A final picture of God that I love is that I am safely shielded under His wings. Remember, you can trust Him to be there for you.

"He who dwells in the shelter of the Most High
Will rest in the shadow of the Almighty.
I will say of the LORD, 'He is my refuge and
My fortress,
My God, in whom I trust.'
Surely he will save you from the fowler's snare
And from the deadly pestilence.
He will cover you with his feathers,
And under his wings you will find refuge;

His faithfulness will be your shield and rampart.
You will not fear the terror of night,
Nor the arrow that flies by day."
(Psalm 91:1-5)

Visualize yourself crawling under those wings—warm, cozy, and secure. He has you in His loving arms.

"...He is my refuge and my fortress,
my God in whom I trust."
(Psalm 91:2)

II. GOD LOVES
Day 13: True Love

The question comes frequently: "Do you love each other?"

That's always a tough one for abuse victims to answer. You want to say, "Of course we love each other." But inside your thoughts, you wonder, "Then why is he so hurtful toward me." Is it hard to "love" someone who abuses you? She THOUGHT she loved him, but now she questions herself.

Actually putting a handle on what "love" is can become very confusing in an abusive relationship. The song goes, "I give to you and you give to me. True love, true love. So on and on it will always be, love forever true." Love is "forever true?" How come it doesn't feel like that?

What is "love" and what is "lust?" Isn't "lust" defined as a feeling, a sudden attraction to somebody you hardly know? "Love" on the other hand is a deep feeling of affection toward a person, arising from kinship and attraction to personal qualities.

With God's love in our lives, we go even deeper still:

"And so we know and rely on the love God has for us.
God is love.
Whoever lives in love lives in God, and God in him."
(I John 4:16)

That simple statement says it all: "GOD IS LOVE." So if we are to find true love, we must connect to God. And it is God's love that empowers us to love others, just as they are.

"Dear friends, let us love one another, for love comes
from God. Everyone who loves has been born of God
and knows God. Whoever does not love does not know
*God, because **God is love.**"* (emphasis mine)
(I John 4:7-8)

And we are also admonished HOW to love:

"Dear friends, let us not love with words or tongue
but with actions and in truth."
(I John 3:18)

So love is much more than words! It's much more than a physical, emotional attraction. True love goes deep, starting with embracing the love of God. Our actions will show that we love "in truth." God's Word gives us a straight definition of what love should look like:

"Love is patient, love is kind.
It does not envy, it does not boast,
it is not proud.
It is not rude, it is not self-seeking,
it is not easily angered,
and it keeps no record of wrongs.
Love does not delight in evil but rejoices with the truth.
It always protects, always trusts, always hopes,
always perseveres.
Love never fails."
(I Corinthians 13:4-8)

This definition is very sobering to me. It feels like the exact OPPOSITE of what happens in an abusive relationship.

God's Love	Abusive Actions
Patient	Impatient
Kind	Cruel
Not envious	Extreme jealousy
No boasting	Intimidating
Not proud	Dominating
Not rude	Verbal put-downs
Not self-seeking	Self-centered
Not easily angered	Explosive anger
No record of wrongs	Condemns your failings
Truth	Evil Distortions
Protects	Threatens
Hopes	Uncertainty
Perseveres	Abandonment
Love never fails	Extreme mood swings

So does "love" mean we hang around for someone to beat us up over and over again—verbally, emotionally, physically? Absolutely not! Showing real love for the abuser is for the victim to take some steps to STOP his torments and compulsions to hurt. It is not helping him by allowing him to continue in irrational and aggressive behavior. Unless this temper is brought under control, it will not only escalate but will affect many other people.

If we are filled with God's Spirit, with a desire in our hearts to live His way, He gives us the strength and power to *"Follow the way of love..."* (I Corinthians 14:1). We cannot control what someone else does or does not do, but we CAN control how WE want to live. *"We know that we live in him and he in us, because he has given us of his Spirit"* (I John 4:13). And the fruit of his Spirit living in us produces a changed life. The *"Acts of the sinful nature..."* (Galatians 5:19) are replaced:

> *"But the fruit of the Spirit is*
> *love, joy, peace, patience, kindness,*
> *goodness, faithfulness, gentleness and self-control.*
> *Against such things there is no law.*
> *Those who belong to Christ Jesus have crucified the*
> *sinful nature with its passions and desires.*
> *Since we live by the Spirit, let us keep in step*
> *with the Spirit."*
> (Galatians 5:22-25)

Without God, love may just be a shallow connection with another person. If the relationship is consumed with self-centered indulgence, it may not actually be "love" at all. Filling our lives with the Holy Spirit is the first step in experiencing real love, and then we can love others as God has loved us—unconditionally. There is no deeper love.

So when I am asked that question, "Do you still love each other?" I have to be honest and say, "I really don't know."

"But the fruit of the Spirit is love. . ."
(Galatians 5:22)

II. GOD LOVES

Day 14: Marriage—A Picture

The union of marriage is given in part to demonstrate God's unconditional love for us. We, in the church, are called his "bride." And Jesus comes to the wedding as the "Lamb."

> *"Let us rejoice and be glad*
> *And give him glory!*
> *For the wedding of the Lamb has come,*
> *And his bride has made herself ready."*
> (Revelation 19:7-9)

We are His bride! Doesn't that make you feel good? Nothing could be more perfect than an intimate union with Jesus Christ Himself. At the end of time in the wedding of the Lamb, He takes us (His believers) as His bride!

In Ephesians 4:22-33, the glorious picture of Christ's love for his church, the bride, is pictured as parallel to the relationship between a husband and wife. The husband loves his wife so much that he would lay down his life to save her (as Jesus did for the church). The husband feeds and cares for her (as Jesus cares for the church) just as he would his own body (and surely he knows how to care for himself). In turn, wives look to the husband as the head of the union (as Christ is the head of the church). She also performs her role as "helpmate," and is safe in his hands because he loves her as he loves himself.

It is truly easy to submit to godly leadership from a husband who totally respects and cares for you. That is God's plan for an ideal marriage.

Sadly, no human marriage can measure up to the perfect union we have with Christ. Picturing Christ as the "husband" and the church as the "bride," there is a complete "marriage." A human marriage means we are *"one in the flesh"* (Genesis 2:24). A union with Christ means we are *"one in spirit"* as we are *"all baptized by one Spirit into one body"* (I Corinthians 12:13). We are One with him.

It was in the final prayer of Jesus that He prayed we would not only be "one" with Him, but also one with each other.

*"Holy Father, protect them by the power of your name— the name you gave me— so that they may be **one as we are one**.*
(emphasis mine)
"While I was with them,
I protected them and kept them safe
by that name you gave me."
(John 17:11-12).

"*I protected them and kept them safe.*" I like that. Being one with Christ means that we have His divine protection.

We can also relish in the fact that God Almighty totally rejoices over us. He loves us, and His love extends as far as the "*heavens are above the earth, so great is his love for those who fear him*" (Psalm 103:11). Soak in His love for you!

"As a bridegroom rejoices over his bride, so will your God rejoice over you."
(Isaiah 62:5b)

That's a beautiful picture of marriage—a bride-groom rejoicing over his bride.

But not every marriage ends that way. Even in the Old Testament, God gave Moses a *"writ of divorce"* (Deuteronomy 24:1-4). We don't know the circumstances when a divorce was allowed in the Old Testament, but it was allowed. Moses would make the judgment call. It is the sinful world we are in. God knew sin in some cases would prevail, and He allowed divorce in certain circumstances.

When the Pharisees questioned Jesus about divorce, He said:

> *"Moses permitted you to divorce your wives*
> *because your hearts were hard.*
> *But it was not this way from the beginning.*
> *I tell you that anyone who divorces his wife,*
> *except for marital unfaithfulness,*
> *and marries another woman commits adultery."*
> (Matthew 1:8-9)

The marriage covenant is a serious oath, made before God, and not to be taken lightly by committing adultery. If a man divorces his wife just to marry someone else, that is condemned.

Paul also expanded the doctrine by saying that if an unbelieving husband wants to leave that you are to let him go!

"But if the unbeliever leaves, let him do so.
A believing man or woman is not bound in such
circumstances;
God has called us to live in peace."
(I Corinthians 7:15)

If he leaves, her goal in life is not to find another husband. Rather Paul suggests that she redirect her life from devotion to a husband to serving God.

"Her aim is to be devoted to the Lord
in both body and spirit."
(I Corinthians 7:34b)

When both husband and wife put obedience to Jesus first, the chances are greater that the marriage will blossom and flourish. Truly God says, *"I hate divorce"* (Malachi 2:16). But in that same verse it assumes that the marriage may be over due to violence.

"You have broken faith with her,
though she is your partner,

the wife of your marriage covenant.
So guard yourself in your spirit,
and do not break faith with the wife of your youth. . .
"I hate divorce. . .and I hate a man's covering himself
with violence
as well as with his garment,
says the Lord Almighty."
(Malachi 2:14 – 16)

It is implied here that the marriage has become a battleground of violence. God clearly hates the violence. He hates when the marriage covenant is violated and destroyed. Yes, He hates divorce, but He also hates the violence. It may be assumed that some marriages will end in divorce due to violence of a husband toward his wife. I agree. I hate that there is violence, and I hate that there is divorce. It's not God's divine plan for marriage.

In this sinful world, humans can break the covenant, but Jesus never will. Never, ever! We are secure in the love of Jesus for us.

"His love endures forever." (Psalm 136:1)

II. GOD LOVES

Day 15: Bride of Christ

P icture yourself at a wedding. It's not a dream; it's truth! You are the Bride of Christ. Jesus Christ—the lover of your soul.

You are dressed and ready for your union. You are clothed in white as he has cleansed you from all sin.

> *"Though your sins are like scarlet,*
> *They shall be as white as snow;*
> *Though they are red as crimson,*
> *They shall be like wool."*
> (Isaiah 1:18b)

You prepare yourself for intimacy as he delights in your presence:

"How delightful is your love, my sister, my bride!

How much more pleasing is your love than wine,
And the fragrance of your perfume than any spice!
Your lips drop sweetness as the honeycomb, my bride;
Milk and honey are under your tongue.
The fragrance of your garments is like
that of Lebanon."
(Song of Songs 4:10-11)

The procession begins:

"They will walk with me, dressed in white,
for they are worthy.
He who overcomes will, like them, be dressed in white.
I will never blot out his name from the Book of Life,
but will acknowledge his name before
my Father and his angels."
(Revelation 4b-5)

You meet your Lover in purity:

Paul writes, *"I promised you to one husband, to Christ,*
so that I might present you as a pure virgin to him."
(2 Corinthians 11:2).

You open your heart and soul to receive His love:

"O God, you are my God,
Earnestly I seek you;
My soul thirsts for you,
My body longs for you,
In a dry and weary land
Where there is no water...
I have seen you in the sanctuary
And beheld your power and your glory.
Because your love is better than life,
My lips will glorify you.
I will praise you as long as I live,
And in your name I will lift up my hands."
(Psalm 63:1-4)

The day will come when we shall see our Loving Savior unveiled, face to face.

"But we know that when he appears,
we shall be like him, for we shall see him as he is.
Everyone who has this hope in him purifies himself,
just as he is pure."
(I John 3:2-3)

We can wait patiently for the wedding to begin, for the marriage supper of the Lamb to come.

"Hallelujah!
For our Lord God Almighty reigns.
Let us rejoice and be glad
And give him glory!
For the wedding of the Lamb has come,
And his bride has made herself ready.
Fine linen, bright and clean,
Was given her to wear.

Then the angel said to me, 'Write:
Blessed are those who are invited
To the wedding supper of the Lamb!'
And he added, 'These are the true words of God.'"
(Revelation 19:6b-9)

When will this be? Nobody knows, but the day WILL come when Jesus returns for His own.

"Keep watch, because you do not know the day
or the hour." (Matthew 25:13)

We are always looking, always expecting His return. And while we are here, we will continue to serve him:

"Therefore, my dear brothers, stand firm.

Let nothing move you.
Always give yourselves fully to the work of the Lord,
because you know that your labor in the Lord is not
in vain."
(I Corinthians 15:58)

Maybe you have serious doubts about your human marriage. Most abuse victims are cajoled into a quick marriage or sexual intimacy soon after meeting. It feels like passionate love to her; but to him, he doesn't want to let her slip away. She is in his grip.

In a dysfunctional marriage, abusive elements will begin early. The wedding day is truly a beautiful day—beautiful dresses, flowers, candles, music, cake, gifts. But the glow of the wedding may quickly dim. This earthly wedding will pale in contrast to the wedding supper of the Lamb (Revelation 19:9).

As a contrast to being clothed in the pure whiteness and beauty of a bride, the darkness creeps in as abuse enlarges. (I was amazed to discover upon opening the box with my wedding dress that it was covered with mold.) The abuser tries to keep the sordid truth silent, but God truly sees it, and He hates it. An abuser tries to hide his actions, which are full of violence. He cloaks the secret, like pulling a garment over himself for a cover.

"'...and I hate a man's covering himself with violence
as well as with his garment,' says the Lord Almighty.
So guard yourself in your spirit, and do not break
faith."
(Malachi 2:16b)

THIS is what God hates, *"a man's covering himself with violence."* It is no wonder that violence breaks faith with the wife of his youth.

Pull next to Jesus and wait for the completeness that will come at the wedding supper of the Lamb, when he takes us as His bride in heaven. THAT will be pure love! No violence! No fear! No hurts!

If marriage has disappointed you deeply here on earth, remember that the love of Jesus is there for you in a deeper, more complete way. Marriage CAN be good here, but only if both partners are filled with devoted love for Jesus and His ways. Even in the best of marriages, realizing true love can and will only come out of a love relationship with Jesus, who is the source of love. Marriage should be a picture of a loving union, but it will always fall short of the glory of God.

Our relationship with Christ is complete. Abide in the thought that there is a pure wedding ahead with our loving Savior, Jesus.

> *". . .your love is better than life. . .I will praise you as long as I live."* (Psalm 63:4)

Day 16: God Created a Woman

As a woman, I am God's final creation in a magnanimous universe. I am the most precious and final jewel in his crown. I have a purpose. I have a goal. I have a specific place in God's world. I am created to be the "glory of man" (I Corinthians 11:7b). And the Lord has given me the most protected spot in the order. My husband is over me for protection, and God is over him. That's secure!

The Lord gives a line of authority as an organizational plan for smooth functioning in our relationships. When things get out of this order, the door opens for dysfunction. This order gives the woman a covering, a very "safe" place to be.

"Now I want you to realize
that the head of every man is Christ,

and the head of the woman is man,
and the head of Christ is God."
(I Corinthians 11:3)

God is at the top, then Christ, then the man, then the woman. When this order is in place, it works!

"Husbands, in the same way be considerate as you live
with your wives,
and treat them with respect as the weaker partner
and as heirs with you of the gracious gift of life,
so that nothing will hinder your prayers."
(I Peter 3:7)

So the woman has all those layers over her. Is it to subdue her and control her? This verse clearly says the husband is to be "considerate" and "treat them with respect." And the penalty for NOT being considerate or NOT treating them with respect is severe. Otherwise, it will *"hinder your prayers."* God has surely set up a system in which women are protected and valued. It's not a "put down." It's an overwhelming system of protection. And men are, in fact, called to a higher calling in how they treat their wives. They answer directly to the authority over them—Christ Himself!

I don't have any trouble accepting the "weaker partner" picture. Just look at the constitution of a man compared to the lesser muscle mass of a woman. Women have the strength and fortitude to deliver a child through immense discomfort, but sometimes we need a man to open a jar. Personally, I do not stumble over the word "weaker."

"Weak" does not mean weak in my mind, weak in my emotions, weak in my knowledge, weak in my wisdom, weak in my spiritual depth, weak in my relationships. "Weak" to me means my body! And I accept the loving covering of a man who protects me with the endowed strength of his body. It's great to go to a strong man to work out the problems of life.

It does not make me feel "inferior" or "inept." On the contrary, the very fact that a man NEEDS a "helpmate" (Genesis 2:18) or helper, means that the man will benefit from his wife's input in a myriad of ways. She assists him in his thinking and in his decisions. Both husband and wife together bring a balanced approach. One is not "better" than the other.

However, some men need to feel "superior" and "in charge" and can become like a "bully" over a woman. That is not God's plan. We have equality in his sight. In God's view, Jesus looks at each of us as the same—One in Christ. There is not a verse of scripture that even hints that God has favored men as opposed to women. It should be a complimentary union.

> *"You are all sons of God through faith in Christ Jesus.*
> *For all of you who were baptized into Christ*
> *have clothed yourselves with Christ.*
> *There is neither Jew nor Greek, slave nor free,*
> *male nor female for you are all one in Christ Jesus."*
> (Galatians 3:26-28)

Additionally, not only did Jesus share some of his most precious moments with women (like His resurrection from the dead John 20), but he also sets the tone for total consideration and respect. Jesus didn't dominate women, looking at them as his "servants." In fact, he said all of us are to *"serve one another in love"* (Galatians 5:13).

If you may entertain the thought that you are "inferior" to a man, look at all the qualities of the woman in Proverbs chapter 31. Look at her list of talents and gifts. What was her character like? Was she respected by her husband?

> *"A wife of noble character who can find?*

She is worth far more than rubies.
Her husband has full confidence in her
And lacks nothing of value.
She brings him good, not harm
All the days of her life."
(Proverbs 31:10-12)

"Charm is deceptive, and beauty is fleeting;
But a woman who fears the Lord is to be praised.
Give her the reward she has earned,
And let her works bring her praise at the city gate."
(Proverbs 31:30-31)

"Her children arise and call her blessed;
Her husband also, and he praises her . . ."
(Proverbs 31:28)

The key to the success of this woman is that she is a woman "who fears the Lord." She looks to the Lord for the substance of her life. And this enables her to serve her husband, her children, and her community with a balance. How special it must be for a husband to praise her.

Yes, God created me, a woman! I'm not inferior, I'm not subservient, I'm not secondary. As the crowning glory of His creation, I am beautiful. Lift your head high and praise God for who you are! And let NO ONE take that picture away from you.

> *"...a woman who fears the LORD is to be praised."* (Proverbs 31:30)

II. GOD LOVES

Prayer of God's Love

Father, you show your greatest love for me
By sending your Son to die in my place.
As if I were the only person left on earth,
I am important to you.
You surround me with perfect and complete love.
Love without fear, love without shame,
love without judgment.
Father, you reach out to me, TO ME, personally.
You call my name,
You know me inside and out.
You protect me and provide for me.
Father, your love is all I need.
Help me to love others as you have loved me, with no
strings attached.
Father, please feel my love for you.
May our relationship get even closer
as we walk this earth together.
I love you!
Amen

Section III

Abuse Hurts

I believe abusing others is a sin.

I believe it is within righteousness

to confront abuse in any form.

I believe I am not dependent on an abuser

but can stand strong against this sin

with God as my strength.

III. ABUSE HURTS

Day 17: Enabling Another

Enabling an abuser is a huge problem. Is it? Isn't the abuse worse? Actually the abuse would STOP if the enabler would stop allowing it. Both conditions—abuser and enabler—make this very dangerous relationship continue.

How does the enabler feed the abuse? It's the same as driving the getaway car for someone who is robbing a bank. It's the same as signing checks when she KNOWS the money is not in the bank. It's the same as turning her back on her own children, even if they are being abused.

An enabler keeps her mouth shut in the midst of wrong. An enabler goes along with lies. She allows her abuser to continue with dirty deeds, not only against her but also against others.

Why is this? Why does an enabler continue to support an abuser? Simply because she has been manipulated to think it's her duty to support her abuser. She doesn't think for herself as her thoughts are being controlled. You might call it "emotional brain-washing." She is in the habit of abiding by HIS rules, and believes he will overpower her if she dares to disagree with him. He doesn't listen to her anyway.

Sometimes an enabler doesn't realize she is in an abusive relationship. In my case I had a very strong father (and very weak mother) and I was used to a male telling me what to do. When I married, I simply transferred that poor emotional attachment to my husband. "Husbands know best," you know. I believed it. And I never "grew up" to think for myself as an adult. I actually had a very hard time expressing my feelings—to anybody.

After maturing and seeing things differently, I gradually began to question the control my husband had over me. Does he really control all the money, all our friends, where we go, and what we do? Why does he resent me (and punish me) for wanting to do something by myself? Why do I feel entrapped in almost every area of my life? Do I really need his permission to do what I want to do?

It came to a climax after repeated foreclosures when I finally said, "No more."

Was it a dangerous thing for me to do? Yes! Because standing up against an abuser can trigger a response from him that could have horrible outcomes. Before standing up to an abuser, it is extremely important to find a support group of people who are committed to helping you. I found an advocacy group of domestic abuse survivors, and they gave me excellent guidance.

We can learn from David in the Old Testament how to stand up to an abuser. David is an example of what we can do when attacked by an enemy. King Saul was out to defeat and even kill David because of an extreme sense of jealousy. When David killed Goliath the Philistine (1 Samuel 17-18), he returned home to great praise from the people:

". . .the women came out from all the towns of Israel
to meet King Saul with singing and dancing,
with joyful songs and with tambourines and lutes.
As they danced, they sang: 'Saul has slain his thou-
sands, and David his tens of thousands."
(I Samuel 18:6-7)

*"The next day an evil spirit from God came
forcefully upon Saul."*
(I Samuel 18:10)

In his evil state, Saul actually tried to kill David by his own hand as he hurled a spear at David, saying :

"'I'll pin David to the wall.' But David eluded him twice."
(I Samuel 18:11)

After numerous unsuccessful attempts to kill David, Saul came to the conclusion that he would remain David's enemy for the rest of his days (I Samuel 18:29). Did David fight back? No. In fact, he separated himself and stayed away from Saul, his enemy. At one point David came so close to Saul while he was sleeping that he had the opportunity to cut a corner off of Saul's robe (I Samuel 13:1-11). David could have killed Saul at that moment. But instead, David retreated, holding this piece of cloth in his hands, proving he was there, yet giving Saul mercy.

With an abusive husband, we can have the same reaction as David. We separate ourselves, we stay away, we retreat, we find a safe place. We will not allow the abuse to continue. We don't need to strike back. But shouldn't we try to defend ourselves? The answer is: God is here to defend us:

> *"If it is possible, as far as it depends on you,*
> *Do not repay anyone evil for evil.*
> *Be careful to do what is right in the eyes of everybody.*
> *Live at peace with everyone.*
> *Do not take revenge, my friends,*
> *but leave room for God's wrath, for it is written:*
> *'It is mine to avenge; I will repay,' says the Lord."*
> (Romans 12:17-19)

Abuse is sin. And allowing hurt and abuse to endlessly continue is enabling that sin. Are we not told to "live at peace with everyone?" Hurting and bullying another person is not part of that picture. Abuse goes against anything and everything that Jesus taught.

If and when we separate from the abuser, he is given two choices:

1. Admit there are deep problems and commit to making some changes with therapy.
2. Reject her even more, and continue a path of hurts toward her.

For the victim, stepping back from the turmoil (which can difficult) should give her a chance to evaluate herself. Why is she so easily victimized? Why is it hard for her to express her feelings? Why was she seduced into this relationship in the beginning? What are her gifts and talents? Is she realizing WHO she really is?

Some women, sadly, go back to an abuser before any serious therapy is done. Why does she go back? It feels comfortable, what she is used to. She feels afraid to face life without him. He overwhelms her with promises and gifts. He makes her feel guilty for causing such a turmoil. He threatens her that "bad things" will happen if she doesn't come back. But regretfully, most women who prematurely go back are only faced with the same abuse, only intensified. He learned something. He knows what to do to get her back. And he knows she is so weak that she will eventually come back. He HAS HER in his grip.

So it takes a VERY strong stature to stand up to an abuser. Other people in the family and other acquaintances can make it more difficult. They may make a judgment call, like, "I never saw him abuse her." So if they didn't see, it doesn't happen? Truth says that most acts of abuse are done behind closed doors. And the abuser appears to most people as being a "charmer."

He is good at creating a false front. She needs to consult with people who know and understand abusive patterns and give her gentle guidance. When the right time comes, she can make a move with support behind her.

For me, I lost some friends, and I lost closeness with some family members. That's the price. But for me, I am the one who KNOWS THE REALITY. No one else can define what I KNOW. And I stand with Jesus who calls "sin" a "sin."

And Jesus is the One who gives me peace and rest in my soul. He sees it all, and He has promised to lift me up in the midst of my weariness. In short, I live to please Him, not the "naysayers" who think they know what's going on, but don't.

"Come to me, all you who are weary and burdened,
and I will give you rest.
Take my yoke upon you and learn from me,
for I am gentle and humble in heart,
and you will find rest for your souls.
For my yoke is easy and my burden is light."
(Matthew 11:28-29)

I repeat over and over that standing up to abuse should not be done alone. It is essential to have wise counsel from people educated in domestic abuse, and then have a team of people (friends, some family members, a pastor, a group at church) surround you with support. Letting abuse go on and on and on is merely showing that the victim is truly ENABLING the abuser to sin. No more enabling!

In your mind and heart, be convinced that sin must stop! You know what is RIGHT, and abuse is WRONG.

"I fear that there may be quarreling, jealousy, outbursts of anger, factions, slander, gossip, arrogance and disorder. I am afraid that when I come again my God will humble me before you, and I will be grieved over many who have sinned earlier and have not repented of the impurity, sexual sin and debauchery in which they have indulged."
(2 Corinthians 12:20-21)

"Examine yourselves to see whether you are in the faith; test yourselves. Do you not realize that Christ Jesus is in you. . .?
*Now we pray to God that you will not do anything wrong. . . but that you will **do what is right.**. . .*
(emphasis mine)
For we cannot do anything against the truth. . ."

(2 Corinthians 13: 5-8)

My prayer for you is that your abuser will take the high road toward healing. We cannot command him to make the right decisions toward restoration, but we can pray for him to seek God's truth. Abuse is sin. And he is an abuser. Until he comes out of denial and faces this truth, there will be no healing.

But you? Remember David. He separated himself from his abuser as the only place to be safe. Truthfully, as his victim, you are probably the LAST person who can lead your abuser to a healthy relationship. He must deal with himself by himself to find a healthy relationship with mutual respect. Your job is to do your own work for yourself.

"Or do you not know that the unrighteous will not inherit the kingdom of God.
*Do not be deceived: neither the sexually immoral, nor idolaters, nor adulterers, nor men who practice homosexuality, nor thieves, nor the greedy, nor drunkards, nor **abusers**, (emphasis mine) nor swindlers will inherit the kingdom of God.*

And such were some of you. But you were washed, you were sanctified, you were justified in the name of the Lord Jesus Christ and by the Spirit of our God."
(I Corinthians 6:9-11)

" . . .***do what is right***" (2 Corinthians 13:7)

III. ABUSE HURTS

Day 18: Physical Hurts

"**N**o one deserves to be hit." I think this statement would have universal acceptance. Except for the abuser, and except for the victim. The abuser thinks, "She deserves to be hurt because of what she just said." Or maybe it's what she didn't say, or what she did, or didn't do. Maybe it was the look on her face, or some place that she went. Maybe she was late, or maybe she left early. Maybe it was something she was wearing or her shoes weren't right. Maybe she just disagreed, or maybe interjected her own thoughts into a discussion. Or maybe she tried to leave, or filed for divorce.

The back of the hand can come out for a wide variety of controlling reasons. Yes, it's all about an abuser needing full control.

Actually, physical abuse is one of the end results of a deranged abuser. Once the abuse starts, it is a downward spiral as he gets stronger and stronger, and she continues to give in. The risk is that many times physical abuse can silence her forever. An abuser is convinced in his mind that she "deserves" to be hit.

It was actually said in court by my husband, "she deserves it." In other words, in his mind he is fully justified that I should be hurt because I "deserve it." (When that word was spoken in the courtroom, the judge abruptly ended the hearing and gave him an ultimatum. "She deserves it," is what an abuser really thinks, and educated professionals know this.)

The victim can also think she "deserves" to be hit (or kicked, or burned, or choked). She certainly must have said something "wrong." She blames herself for not doing the "right thing." After years of being "defective," sometimes she starts believing the lies, and crawls into the fetal position of submission. He surely knows what is "best." After all she believes, "He's smarter than me."

But then a bruised eye starts to show, and a few stitches are needed. Others see that she dreads going home. Her friends don't understand why she can't ever go out with them. The "secret" gradually comes out.

It's a dangerous time for a victim. She may incite a final outburst of anger with fatal consequences if she dares to speak up and tell someone the truth.

The big problem here is DISHONESTY. She hides the offense, and makes excuses in her mind for the violence that happened. "He was tired" or "He is under so much pressure." He on the other hand will go to extreme measures to hold on to this deception. That's why he wants her to stay HOME, or he follows her when she is going out, or he listens to her conversations on the phone or what she is doing on the email. He is always looking over her shoulder. It keeps her from communicating with others. All of this happens behind closed doors. Out in public, no one would suspect that this couple has a double life. They might look great in the community, but the secrets of the home environment are closely kept. Oftentimes other family members know nothing about the terror, or don't believe it if a little bit of the "secret" slips out.

I was actually told that surely there wasn't any abuse in our family structure because of a strange conclusion. "Look how good your children are." Looking only from the outside of a home doesn't reveal what is actually going on inside.

Do Jesus' words, "turn the other cheek" (Matthew 5:39), mean we have no choice but to walk into a beating, over and over again? Should we strike back in some way? On the contrary, the attitude here is that we are NOT to strike back. We are not to "return evil for evil" (Romans 12:17). That doesn't mean we STAY there.

We are admonished in Romans to "do what is right in the eyes of everybody" (Romans 12:17). Doing what is "right" starts with not believing the lie that a victim "deserves" to be hit. And don't keep it a secret. What is actually "right"? Stopping the sin of abuse! That's what's RIGHT!

We can face the abuse in honesty, we can forgive, but we also must not subject ourselves to endless beatings, verbal or physical, at the whim of an out-of-control abuser. We are to seek to live in PEACE. That means that the abuse is addressed with professionals so that both the abuser and the victim have a choice and a chance for recovery. It also may mean that the victim must separate herself for her own safety while reconciliation is sought.

"Live in harmony with one another. . .
Do not repay anyone evil for evil.

Be careful to do what is right in the eyes of everybody.
If it is possible as far as it depends on you,
live at peace with everyone.
Do not take revenge, my friends,
but leave room for God's wrath, for it is written:
'It is mine to avenge; I will repay' says the LORD."
(Romans 12:16-19)

Jesus has also said that those who are under per-secution will be "blessed":

"Blessed are the peacemakers,
For they will be called sons of God.
Blessed are those who are persecuted because
Of righteousness,
For theirs is the kingdom of heaven.
Blessed are you when people insult you,
Persecute you and falsely say all kinds of evil
against you
Because of me. Rejoice and be glad,
Because great is your reward in heaven."
(Matthew 5:9-12)

I believe the new role of a victim is to minister to the abuser. Yes! Minister to the abuser! He is obviously not living in the way of the Lord. Our first job is to pray for him. At the same time we may need to withdraw from the environment, not out of fear, but out of wisdom. Staying close only continually adds fuel to an already destructive fire.

Do you think you can "change him"? Truthfully, you are probably the LAST person who can affect a change of behavior in him. He uses you, he battles with you, he finds an easy person in you to vent his inner anger, and he certainly is not going to accept any advice from you. You can gently suggest that YOU are going for counseling to find some help and healing for yourself, and you simply encourage him to do the same. It is not your job to find a counselor for him. If he doesn't admit that he needs a counselor himself, then your suggestions are futile.

"Heal thyself" (Luke 4:23)! That's wisdom.

To be perfectly clear, if the facts reveal that one person is abusing another, here are some suggested steps to recovery:

1. **Be honest, coming out of denial.** *("An honest witness tells the truth, but a false witness tells lies,"* Proverbs 12:7.)
2. **Don't keep it a secret, but tell a professional.** *("Speak the truth in love"* Ephesians 4:15.)

3. **Protect yourself from further assaults**. *("Guard your heart"* Proverbs 4:23.)
4. **Pray for peace and harmony**. *("Do not be anxious about anything, but in every situation, by prayer and petition, with thanksgiving, present your requests to God."* Philippians 4:6.)

How long do you wait before you make a move out of the situation? Surely you give the abuser every chance to repent and reconcile. The first step is to carefully call "abuse" ABUSE. If he calls you names, confront it. If he hides the money, tell him you will not live this way. If he hinders your friendships, be considerate of his time but tell him you need time with friends. If he hits you, LEAVE. Only one hit! Never two. Tell him you will not tolerate physical assaults.

Then look at his reaction. Does he take a stronger stand against you, not admitting his violent acts? Or does he show some signs of wanting help? If he agrees to some kind of counseling, take him at his word. You want to see ACTIONS, not mere words. Give him deadlines to make a step toward change.

If these confrontations only make him angrier, then a "safe place" must be found. He is the one who needs to leave. (I made the mistake of being the one who decided to leave, and I never ever was allowed back in the house. His anger intensified, but he showed me who he really was at that point. I didn't want back in.)

"If it is possible as far as it depends on you,
live at peace with everyone."
(Romans 12:18)

III. ABUSE HURTS

Day 19: Verbal Abuse

M any people may think that a slap is the beginning of an abusive cycle. In truth, physical
attacks fall toward the end of the failing relationship.
There are so many other steps that take place in this
downward spiral. Verbal abuse is usually at the beginning. How does a victim handle verbal abuse?

Derogatory remarks set the stage for further control over a victim. She can't believe her ears. "Did he
really say that?" "I don't think he really meant it." "I
need to be more careful not to provoke him next time."

Verbal abuse can rear its ugly head in many forms.
Pat Evans wrote a very insightful book, *The Verbally
Abusive Relationship,* which gives instruction about
this defect. Some examples of verbal abuse are: name
calling, judging, criticizing, trivializing, undermining,
threatening, withholding, making fun at someone

else's expense, accusing, blaming, demeaning. Mostly these approaches are used in the privacy of the home, but the day comes when they are used in public in front of other people.

When verbal abuse is present, anger has become out of control. He cannot get his way by talking in normal tones with a respectful dialogue. So his voice gets louder, and his body gives signs (red face, tight fists, emboldened shoulders, walking toward someone in an intimidating way) that anger is escalating. It's like talking to a fierce tiger that is about to devour you. The tiger doesn't understand a thing except he is ready to attack you. When verbal abuse presents itself in an angry outrage, there can be no further dialogue. The abuser is not only diminishing who you are, but also anything you might say or do. You might be called "ignorant" or "stupid" or "crazy." It is an attempt to weaken the victim, and it makes the abuser feel powerful. He uses his voice and body to hopefully weaken you.

Is this the way of the LORD? That's an easy answer. NO!

"What causes fights and quarrels among you?
Don't they come from your desires that battle
within you?

You want something but don't get it.
You kill and covet, but you cannot have what you want.
You quarrel and fight."
(James 4:1-2)

The tongue can actually hurt deeper than a slap across the face. That is because it is an attack on your personhood, your heart, your soul, your mind. It puts a cut deep in your heart where no bandage can reach. The only way healing can come is through asking forgiveness and seeking reconciliation. Eliminating verbal abuse requires a change of heart, a confession of sin, repentance, and a sincere desire to make a change. Before that, the abuser has to admit that he is guilty of verbal abuse. That won't happen overnight (if at all).

God's Word speaks of the difficulty in changing the habit of verbal abuse.

"When we put bits into the mouths of horses
to make them obey us, we can turn the whole animal.
. . . Likewise the tongue is a small part of the body,
but it makes great boasts.
Consider what a great forest is set on fire by a
small spark.

The tongue also is a fire,
a world of evil among the parts of the body.
It corrupts the whole person,
sets the whole course of his life on fire,
and is itself set on fire by hell.
All kinds of animals, birds, reptiles and creatures of
the sea are being tamed and have been tamed by man,
but no man can tame the tongue.
It is a restless evil, full of deadly poison."
(James 3:3, 5-8)

Strong language:
". . .a world of evil,"
". . .corrupts the whole person,"
". . .restless evil, full of deadly poison."

It is like the abuser sets the victim on fire, to destroy her, to damage her, to control her with words. His words are *"deadly poison,"* damaging and lethal to the heart. Are we to endure name-calling, and the other forms of abuse? Remember, verbal abuse is a solid indicator of an angry and vindictive man.

A sign in an elementary school clarifies behavior that crosses the line of abusing another. It's a warning for us all:

"Violence and/or disrespectful behavior is:
any word, look, sign, or act that hurts a person's
body, possessions, dignity, or security."

And it starts with words! Verbal abuse needs to be recognized and confronted. If it is allowed to burn, it will consume and destroy the relationship. The Lord gives us the opposite as a goal:

"Whatever is true, whatever is noble,
whatever is lovely, whatever is admirable—
if anything is excellent or praiseworthy—
think about such things."
(Philippians 4:8)

That is the way of the LORD. That's God's world. Recognize verbal abuse for what it is—the beginning step in a disintegrating relationship. It's an effort to keep you subservient, doubting yourself, paralyzing you, defeating you. Take a stand against it. You will NOT be talked to that way. Put up your hand in defiance. Leave the room. Refuse to dialogue with verbal abuse. It must either stop, or it will get worse. It's up to you!

"The wisdom that comes from heaven
is first of all pure;
then peace-loving, considerate, submissive,
full of mercy and good fruit, impartial and sincere. . .

"Peacemakers who sow in peace raise a har-
vest of righteousness."

(James 3:17-18).

III. ABUSE HURTS
Day 20: Emotional Abuse

E motional abuse is something that "rocks your boat." The wounding actually goes deeper than physical abuse because it messes with your mind and your feelings, your deepest core. You are at the whim of somebody else's drastic "mood swings." One minute you are here, the next minute you are there. It's the picture of a *"double-minded man, unstable in all he does"* (James 1:8). He is like *"a wave of the sea, blown and tossed by the wind"* (James 1:6). Your mind is scrambled as you try to get a grip on what is really happening. Why all the confusion? Does he love you or does he hate you? It can change from moment to moment.

Psalm 51 (which some call the "abuse Psalm") speaks about the range of emotions that can pervade the victim as she tries desperately to focus on reality.

It can feel like she is being "rung through the ringer" as she never knows where she stands.

> *"My thoughts trouble me and I am distraught*
> *At the voice of the enemy,*
> *At the snares of the wicked;*
> *For they bring down suffering upon me*
> *And revile me in their anger.*
>
> *My heart is in anguish within me;*
> *The terrors of death assail me.*
> *Fear and trembling have beset me;*
> *Horror has overwhelmed me."*
> (Psalm 51:2-5)

And this confusion and fear comes from a lover!

> *"But it is you, a man like myself,*
> *My companion, my close friend*
> *With whom I once enjoyed sweet fellowship*
> *As we walked with the throng*
> *At the house of God."*
> (Psalm 51:13-14)

His clever words compound the terror and insecurity.

> *"My companion attacks his friends;*
> *He violates his covenant.*
> *His speech is smooth as butter,*
> *Yet war is in his heart;*
> *His words are more soothing than oil,*
> *Yet they are drawn swords."*
> (Psalm 51:20-21)

Emotional abuse can be seen in several ways:

- "Crazy-making"—or making you feel like you don't understand what you are saying.
- "Changing the plans"—or altering what you had planned to do, without giving reasons and without considering your thoughts.
- "Twisting words"—taking your language and making it seem like you meant something different than what you said.
- "Lying"—or totally denying that you said or did something, or that he said or did something.
- "Absenteeism"—or failing to show up when you had plans to meet.

- "Holding secrets"—or not sharing vital information with you.

Emotional abuse is the essence of "mood swings," a strong indicator of an unstable personality. She never knows what is really going on. There can be no productive dialogue with this split and perplexing thinking. One minute it is hot, the next minute it is cold. One minute he feels close, the next minute he cuts the rug right out from under your feet. It keeps the victim dangling from a thread, and at the same time makes the abuser feel very much in control.

The victim needs to recognize that this IS what is called "emotional abuse. " He plays with your emotions like a lump of clay, pushing you here and prodding you there at his whim. There is no resolution. Standing up to this confusion may precipitate an angry response, mostly blaming you for all the problems. He may also give you some threats—about leaving you, about destroying possessions, about hitting you, about divorcing you. Remember, that a threat is like saying: "Do what I say or you are dead!" It's all about attacking your emotions and making you feel weak and dependent.

If you recognize this scenario, it is a time once again to consult with a professional abuse-trained counselor. The abuser is controlling you with words! He is wrapping you in chains so you can't move to the right or to the left. He is pushing you under water so you can have no voice. He is locking you in a closet so you can't move. He is trying to remake you into a puppet, controlled by the pull of his strings. Emotional abuse can cripple your mind so that you doubt yourself. It may be helpful to write down the threats that come which leave your emotions dangling. Look at them in the Light of God's ways. If he plays with your emotions, he is an abuser.

Recognize what emotional abuse is—words that deny your feelings and control you with threats. I had to have someone say to me, "That's emotional abuse." I didn't recognize it in my own life. Once I started to write these threats down, I finally started to recognize the pattern of remarks that were made to trample and confuse me. This helped for me to face reality—I was married to an abuser!

Psalm 51 also gives the "rest of the story" and offers a rescue that comes from God.

"But I call to God
And the LORD saves me.

Evening, morning and noon
I cry out in distress,
And he hears my voice.
He ransoms me unharmed
From the battle waged against me,
Even though many oppose me.
God, who is enthroned forever,
Will hear them and afflict them—
Men who never change their ways
And have no fear of God."
(Psalm 51:16-19)

So this is the first move, to go to God and receive the help he promised. His Word states the problem: *"Men who never change their ways and have no fear of God."* That's it! *"No fear of God,"* so they don't care what comes out of their mouth. Emotional abuse is a product of a demented mind, and not to be tolerated.

"Cast your cares on the LORD
And he will sustain you;
He will never let the righteous fall. . .
As for me, I will trust in you."
(Psalm 51:22-23b)

"...I cry out in distress, and he hears my voice." (Psalm 55:17)

III. ABUSE HURTS
Day 21: Financial Abuse

Money can become one of the lethal weapons of an abuser. It is a quiet assault, a bloody stab in the back that no one else can easily see. It leaves the victim helpless and quietly bruised. For the abuser, depriving his victim of money can (in his mind) make her stay with him. It's his chain wrapped around her body.

The first action during the rage of my husband when he discovered that I had left the house was to go to the bank and withdraw all the money. He wanted to make sure that I wouldn't have any money without him. And then maybe I would come back. Because of wise counsel from domestic abuse advocates, I thankfully had saved $3000 for a cushion, not knowing what would happen next. It helped me find an apartment and a lawyer. My husband's first actions after I left made me only more certain that he didn't care about my welfare.

Money can make you feel powerful. The need to have more and more money comes from a persona that needs to APPEAR successful—maybe with a prestigious job, a big house, frequent vacations, and a handsome bank account. As believers we know that riches are not the measure of a man. In fact, Jesus said,

> *"Do not store up for yourselves treasures on earth,*
> *where moth and rust destroy,*
> *and where thieves break in and steal.*
> *But store up for yourselves treasures in heaven,*
> *where moth and rust do not destroy,*
> *and where thieves do not break in and steal.*
> *For where your treasure is,*
> *there your heart will be also."*
> (Matthew 6:19-21)

Money can, if allowed, destroy authentic faith. Where do we look for our security and purpose in life? If we plan on storing up mounds of money for mounds of things, none of this is guaranteed to bring us happiness and fulfillment. In fact, money can take the place of TRUE faith in an Almighty God. We find security in our bank accounts instead of faith in God to supply our needs. Jesus said riches could be a barrier to finding the true meaning in life as it is *"hard for a rich man to enter the kingdom of heaven"* (Matthew 19:23).

What is the end result of focusing on accumulating and hoarding wealth?

"People who want to get rich fall into temptation and a trap and into many foolish and harmful desires that plunge men into ruin and destruction. For the love of money is a root of all kinds of evil. Some people, eager for money, have wandered from the faith and pierced themselves with many griefs."
(I Timothy 6:9-10).

What kind of "ruin and destruction?" An abuser can use money as a weapon of power over a victim. Who pays the bills? Who decides how money is spent? Who has the main role as breadwinner? Does one person make all money decisions? Does he consult his partner? Does he build up debt without her consent? Maybe he prevents her from getting and holding a job. Maybe he makes her ask for money. Maybe she is limited to an allowance. Maybe he secretly helps himself to money she has saved. Maybe he considers all the family's income as belonging only to him.

All of this is control! It leaves the victim feeling helpless and dependent.

Money affects almost every part of our lives—what we eat, where we go, where we live, what we wear. Yes, it pays the bills. But for an abuser, it can become a tool to keep a victim dependent. In fact, most abused women are afraid to leave an abusive husband because of one reason—money. It can come from the abuser's obsessions and insecurities in which he only feels safe when he controls EVERYTHING. He is not interested in what SHE may think. Not in the slightest. That's why he can get rid of her if she bothers him too much. He really doesn't need her. He feels no remorse if she goes away from him. In fact, he may fight for her for a while but only if she comes back under his terms. If she stays away, he will settle into a lifetime of trying to hurt her. His main concern is to take care of himself. How dare she leave him.

Marriage was designed to be a partnership—the two becoming one flesh, one in purpose, one in management. Husbands are not a "daddy" making all the decisions for a little girl. Even the civil law considers a marriage to be 50/50. The assets are shared property, not all his.

The Scriptures give us perspective on how to approach our financial pursuits. We are taught to *"Seek first the kingdom of God and his righteousness, and all these things shall be added unto you"* (Matthew 6:33). When we put the will of God FIRST, everything else falls into place. We are encouraged to live to be RICH in GOOD WORKS:

"Command those who are rich in this present world not
to be arrogant nor to put their hope in wealth, which
is so uncertain, but to put their hope in God, who
richly provides us with everything for our enjoyment.
Command them to do good, to be rich in good deeds,
and to be generous and willing to share.
In this way they will lay up treasure for themselves
as a firm foundation for the coming age,
so that they may take hold of the life that is truly life."
(I Timothy 6:17-19)

Wealth is *"uncertain."* On the other hand, putting our hope in God gives us *"everything"* we need. With this attitude, we can have a desire to be *"generous"* and *"willing to share."* And this gives us a *"firm foundation"* for whatever we face in the present as well as the future. Being *"rich in good deeds"* brings us to a place where we will experience *"the life that is truly life."*

Keeping our focus on the will of God in our lives will bring us a deep sense of contentment. God has promised to give us everything we really need, not everything we may want. Everything we really NEED! He knows best.

If you feel trapped when it comes to the control of money in your life, it is another time to consult some professionals in financial management before the marriage breaks apart. Money is a huge destroyer of marriages. Don't let it creep into your relationship. There needs to be a balance and an oversight concerning the budget. Both husband and wife need to agree about finances. That is a basic tenet of a working partnership.

My dysfunction was thinking my husband was "smarter" than me when it comes to money, so surely he knew how to handle it best. With one foreclosure after another, I finally learned the hard way that this was a total miscalculation. When approaching the topic of finances in counseling, I was dismayed and confounded when he said, "I am a private person, and

I'm not willing to share with her or anybody." Really? What kind of marriage is this!

Managing money in marriage needs to be a total partnership. If you feel like you have no freedom with your own money, or maybe you are prevented from working for some money, or maybe he never is willing to give you a dime, then please take these issues to a counselor for some sound advice. The balance is not there. He is holding money over your head to keep you dependent on him, controlling everything again. When his credit rating affects your credit rating, that is a stab in the back, especially if you were not given any opportunity to know or discuss the family finances. (I learned this the hard way.)

I have often wondered if our marriage would have ended differently if we had had some financial counseling before we were married. But there was no turning back. Now I know that a true partnership includes agreement about financial decisions. And his secrecy and control of all the money reveals a distorted view of marriage.

At this point I have learned not to be dependent upon him for anything—not money, not possessions, not housing, not income. I am better managing my own finances where there is HONESTY, not deception.

"But godliness with contentment is great gain.
For we brought nothing into the world,
and we can take nothing out of it.
But if we have food and clothing,
we will be content with that."
(I Timothy 6:6-8)

". . .godliness with contentment is great gain."
(I Timothy 6:6)

III. ABUSE HURTS

Day 22: Sexual Abuse

Wen we think of sexual abuse, the one picture that may come to mind is a priest making physical advances on an unsuspecting altar boy. Or a college student being gang raped after a night of drinking. Or a father sneaking into the bed of his young daughter. But what about a married couple? Can there be sexual abuse in a marriage?

Sexual abuse is defined as NOT consensual—one party dominates the level of sexual intercourse over the victim. For some reason, the victim feels powerless to stop it. She succumbs to physical demands, out of a state of helplessness or weakness. Afterwards she feels not only guilty but ashamed. "Why did I let him do that?" "Why didn't I stand up for myself?" "It feels like he is just using my body for his own desires." "He doesn't really care about me or what I feel."

Sexual abuse in marriage can mean that she pulls herself under the covers, not knowing what is going to happen next. She might be awakened at 3:00 in the morning, without a word, and expected to "enjoy" the interaction. She might be told in the morning that the sexual experience was "not good for him." She feels conflicted in her mind about sex. It IS a part of marriage. Why then doesn't she feel sexually fulfilled? Why doesn't it feel like "love"? Why is it so frequent, but yet her feelings are ignored? Why can't she simply say "no?" Why does he continue to do things during the sexual experience that she detests? Why does he tell her "dirty" jokes, or show her porn pictures of other women? Why does he need to watch sexually explicit movies when she is in the room?

Most of all, why don't they ever talk about sex together? She knows for sure that *"the spirit is willing but the body is weak"* (Matthew 26:41). With one touch she seems to melt and becomes defenseless. She's confused about what to do, or what not to do. It doesn't feel right. Sex should be a part of marriage, but this?

God is the author of sex! It is given to us to be a blessing in life. It is very clear in Scripture that God has also warned us against degrading sexual pursuits. It can come in many ways:

"Do you not know that the wicked will not inherit the
kingdom of God?
Do not be deceived:
Neither the sexually immoral nor idolaters
nor adulterers nor male prostitutes nor homosexual
offenders nor thieves nor the greedy nor drunkards
nor slanderers nor swindlers
will inherit the kingdom of God.
And that is what some of you were.
But you were washed, you were sanctified,
you were justified
in the name of the Lord Jesus Christ and
by the Spirit of our God.
. . . . The body is not meant for sexual immorality,
but for the Lord, and the Lord for the body.
. . . . Do you not know that he who unites himself with a
prostitute is one with her in body?
For it is said, 'the two will become one flesh.'
But he who unites himself with the Lord is one with
him in spirit.
Flee from sexual immorality.
All other sins a man commits are outside his body,
but he who sins sexually sins against his own body.
Do you not know that your body is a temple of the
Holy Spirit,

who is in you, whom you have received from God?
You are not your own; you were bought at a price.
Therefore honor God with your body."
(I Corinthians 6:9-20)

That's a list of how sex can be abused, or performed out of God's will. *"Sexually immoral...adulterers...male prostitutes...homosexuals...prostitutes."* And this perversion is called a sin against a man's own body. He hurts HIMSELF!

The sexual union was meant to be a loving act between two people who have been joined together in spirit, and now are joined together in the flesh. *"The two shall become one flesh."* Any distortion of this design is called *"sexually immoral."*

In God's world, pure love should mean pure sex. Immoral love is simply an act of selfishness, one meeting his own needs with no regard for his partner. In truth, there should be no fear in the relationship:

"There is no fear in love.
But perfect love drives out fear,
because fear has to do with punishment.
The one who fears is not made perfect in love."
(I John 4:18)

If immoral love is self-indulgent, then the opposite is also true. God's love is selfless. And there is no fear! If you want a glimpse of God's unending and enduring love, read the *Song of Songs* in the Bible. It not only reflects an image of true human love, but also a parallel of God's love for us, His bride.

> *" . . .For love is as strong as death,*
> *Its jealousy unyielding as the grave.*
> *It burns like blazing fire,*
> *Like a mighty flame.*
> *Many waters cannot quench love;*
> *Rivers cannot wash it away."*
> (Song of Songs 8:6b-7a)

Truly sex should be a close and intimate part of a marriage, one in which both are cognizant of the needs and desires of the other. Love means putting others ahead of yourself. Love is never a place to instill fear or intimidation. When sexual interactions are done out of a purely selfless motive, love can be felt in a deep and beautiful way. Do it God's way, out of a selfless heart.

> *". . .For love is as strong as death,"*
> (Song of Songs 8:6b).

III. ABUSE HURTS
Day 23: Intimidation

All abuse is an effort at intimidation—one person attempting to overpower another person. It can come through a variety of means—physical, verbal, emotional, financial, sexual, and even spiritual. The abuser makes an attempt to put fear in the heart of a victim. Then he becomes powerful and controls the relationship, like a bully. She is intimidated, and that's what he wants.

What is it that would frighten you? Smashing possessions? Slanderous words? Making threats? Throwing things? Taking all the money? Hurting a pet? Slamming fists on the wall or a table? Backing you into a corner? Displaying a weapon? Hitting or kicking? Disappearing?

What if the abuser controls what you do, where you go? How about whom you see and talk to? What if he demands that you stay home?

This is the life of the abused.

Of course the abuser will never admit that he is guilty of any sort of intimidation. He views himself as "the boss." In fact, he will make light of the control and not take any of her concerns seriously. He may even laugh at her concerns, or act like she is crazy in her thinking. He easily blames her for anything that goes wrong. He has all the power!

She may dread crawling into bed at night, or getting up in the morning, or coming home from a day at work. She doesn't know who to talk to. Who would ever believe her stories? In public they may look like a perfectly happy couple. Her husband totally appears to be a "nice guy."

This is the life of an abused woman. She feels trapped and uncertain about her life. She lives in a fearful pattern of intimidation and control in the relationship, sometimes for years. It's like the frog in a kettle that is heated by a burner. The gradual heat of the fire slowly creeps up, finally to the point of killing the frog. He could have jumped out, but his senses were accustomed to the environment. And he was dulled in his thinking to make any attempt to escape.

Furthermore, the fear of trying to put a stop to a husband's abuse may have disastrous consequences. The fear keeps her motionless! What will he do if his anger is triggered? How can she find money to meet her daily needs if she doesn't get it from him? Where would she go? Should she insist that he is the one who needs to leave? How would he react to that?

No easy answers. But that is why the downward spiral of a deteriorating relationship should not be ignored. The victim needs to find some support from abuse counselors before taking any major steps. The narcissistic and self-indulgent abuser won't have an easy fix as the problems go deep to his core, way back to early childhood. Sometimes an abuser hits bottom and is willing to seek out some therapy. Actually, both the victim and the abuser need therapy to ease the compulsions that drive them. In-depth Christian counseling is the only path to complete recovery.

Intimidation is a summary word for the meaning of "abuse." "Bully" could be another word. So how is an intimidating relationship contrary to God's will?

First of all, one person does not BELONG to another. We are God's! And we are to answer to Him for the course of our lives. It's nice to be able to partner with another as we walk through this life.

But what if the husband is clearly an unbeliever? That only means trauma is ahead. The oneness in the Spirit just won't be there. God has given us the warning.

"Do not be yoked together with unbelievers.
For what do righteousness and wickedness have in common?
Or what fellowship can light have with darkness?
What harmony is there between Christ and (Satan)?
What does a believer have in common
with an unbeliever?
...Therefore come out from them and be separate."
(2 Corinthians 6:14-17)

It can be a very difficult life to enter into marriage with an unbeliever. For that reason, the courtship time should be a time of rigid testing and seeking God's will. Allegiance to the Lord should be FIRST. Both should feel a oneness in spirit about putting God first.

"For none of us lives to himself alone
and none of us dies to himself alone.
If we live, we live to the Lord;

and if we die, we die to the Lord.
So, whether we live or die, we belong to the Lord."
(Romans 14:7-8)

It may be extremely confusing if the husband claims to be a "believer." Maybe you have gone to church together for years. And in church you may look like the ideal couple. Why don't you feel close in your spiritual lives? I know this is one area I ignored after meeting my husband. I just noticed he went to church, but we never talked about it. Truthfully, I was enjoying the fun and didn't want anything to mess it up. I realized only too soon that we were really "not on the same page" spiritually. I had difficulty even trying to bring up anything about our faith.

If finding a oneness in spirit is of primary importance, how then do we know a "true" believer? Jesus says, *"By their fruits, you shall know them"* (Matthew 7:20). In other words, look at their lives. Do their acts fall within the commands of Christ? Do they give praise and thanks to God for their existence? Let us be clear here. It is not our role to judge someone's relationship with God. We never tell someone, "You are not a Christian." That is not our role. But He also admonishes us to "watch out."

"Watch out for false prophets.
They come to you in sheep's clothing,
but inwardly they are ferocious wolves.
By their fruit you will recognize them.
Do people pick grapes from thorn bushes, or figs from
thistles?
Likewise every good tree bears good fruit, but a bad
three bears bad fruit.
. . .Thus, by their fruit you will recognize them.
(Matthew 7:16-20)

It says, "recognize them." That doesn't mean it is our role to condemn them. So if we see godless acts and clear disobedience to scripture, then we can have reason to doubt. Jesus did warn us about these "false prophets." But in all wisdom, there should never be a marriage unless there is NO DOUBT about the level of faith in Christ. This oneness is absolutely the most important union, to be "one in spirit."

A marriage "made in heaven" means that two people come together with common respect for each other. They have a found a compatibility in purpose and faith. They each have their roles on how to serve God, and they support each other. God gives them every tool they need to live in peace, as long as they earnestly seek Him. It is definitely a plus if they are able to share scripture together and pray together. A spiritual unity should bring both together in a deeper aura of peace, respect, and love.

"Let us therefore make every effort to do what leads to peace and to mutual edification."
(Romans 14:19)

"...God has called us to live in peace."
(I Corinthians 6:15b)

Day 24: Spiritual Abuse

We've all heard the stories. A priest takes advantage of his position of authority by sexually abusing unsuspecting young boys. No one can doubt it. It's called "spiritual abuse," or using his power as a spiritual leader to intimidate others. Most of us implicitly trust our spiritual leaders. We give them due respect and listen to their words of guidance. Surely they are close to God, and wouldn't do anything "wrong."

But there are times when this authority is abused and ends up hurting others. Spiritual leaders may step outside of their boundaries, and even outside the Scripture. It's hard to confront a spiritual leader and say, "That's not right!" Spiritual abuse can result in deep hurt, sometimes the deepest of hurts as it hits the heart and soul of the core of our being.

As a prime example, when I was holding a restraining order in my hands to protect me from my enraged husband, the church told me to sit in the back row of the sanctuary. Then after the service, I was told by the elders to "take a break" from church until we worked out our "problems." I guess they didn't want to have a "scene" at church. We (both my husband and I) were asked not to come back to the church community until we met with the elder board and obtained their "permission."

What? I had just lost my husband, my house, my money, my job (as I worked at the church), and now my church family? As I exited this church, I suggested that they were "kicking the wounded." Why would anyone fail to feel compassion for a woman holding a restraining order? Without the backing of my church, I was thrown into an even deeper state of confusion. I know now that they were misled, and without a doubt were functioning out of the boundaries of Scripture.

It wasn't long before God led me to a very supportive church with an empathetic pastor who welcomed me with the compassion and love of Jesus. It resulted in eventually starting a ministry to the abused in this new church. Praise to God!

(Side note: Two years later with a new pastor, the first church offered an apology to me for their treatment of both my husband and me. Hopefully, some deep lessons were learned.)

But the contrast between these two churches taught me that we have a serious and woefully lacking outlook about the dynamics of abuse that can exist within the church community. It DOES happen in the church. I am proof! We sat in the pew together for years, many times with his arm around my shoulders. The church became the place to give us the false front that we were a fine Christian family. I was VERY hesitant to share my turmoil with anyone in church. Would they believe me?

So I know and have felt spiritual abuse. I was judged, I was condemned, I was abandoned, I was threatened, I was forgotten BY THE CHURCH! Does this sound like the hands and feet of Jesus?

Yes, people sin, even in the church. *"All of us have sinned, and fall short of the glory of God"* (Romans 3:23). Our response is not to judge others caught in a sin. But rather, Galatians tells us what we should do:

"Brothers, if someone is caught in a sin,
you who are spiritual should restore him gently.

But watch yourself, or you also may be tempted.
Carry each other's burdens,
and in this way you will fulfill the law of Christ.
If anyone thinks he is something when he is nothing,
he deceives himself.
Each one should test his own actions."
(Galatians 6: 1-4)

"Restore him gently. . ." That's what we are told to do! We should be giving mercy and compassion and forgiveness and guidance from the Word of God, to both the abused and the abuser. The church is just a group of people who are sinners, but who are forgiven because of the blood of Jesus. We are not perfect. The church should be a body that helps us to grow closer to God and closer to His ways as we serve Him here on earth, throughout the ups and downs of life. We don't kick sinners out, otherwise NO ONE would be there. We should be a group of people who know and understand the unconditional forgiveness of Christ.

During my struggles to survive after first escaping, it was amazing to hear people quote Scripture to me. I know they were trying to be helpful, but none of these verses applied to what I was facing at the moment:

- *"Wives, submit to your husbands."* (Colossians 3:18). (Or, how dare I get a restraining order.)
- *"Blessed are you when people insult you, persecute you and falsely say all kinds of evil against you because of me. Rejoice and be glad. . ."* (Matthew 5:11-12) (Or, just get beat up.).
- *"Do not entertain an accusation against an elder unless it is brought by two or three witnesses"* (I Timothy 5:19). (My husband was an elder.)
- *"'I hate divorce,' says the LORD God of Israel..."* (Malachi 2:16). (In other words, Christians never divorce? Please look at the rest of the verse.)

The truth in my situation was that I was in extreme danger because of the rage of an abuser. Over 25% of women who leave their husbands to escape an abusive environment are murdered! It's an extremely volatile time when a husband is filled with out-of-control wrath. He blames her for everything, and has no feelings of empathy for her situation. He just wants her to STAY, and threatens her if she dares to leave.

It was only after I left that I started to think clearly, with the help of godly counselors. I needed to leave, after having exhausted all resources to seek a peaceful place with my husband. His wrath was escalating by the day. It was not a safe place for me.

Sadly, after I left, my husband's anger only increased dramatically. He could have stopped right then on the same day I left to do something to save our marriage, but he chose to fight me even harder. That wrath continues to this day.

The point here is that the church should be a haven for sinners, a place for forgiveness and reconciliation. Sadly, it is true that churches at times turn their backs on domestic abuse problems. "We don't know what to do," I have been told. "Do you think you are exaggerating?" "We've never seen him become angry." They may make quick judgments with harsh accusations, which only worsens the situation. It is true that they probably DON'T understand domestic abuse. That is why the church should have a plan ahead of time, and partner with the professionals in the community who have the experience and the knowledge to deal with this highly volatile situation.

One added fact is that more police are killed while responding to domestic abuse situations than any other. It is a highly potent situation and can have disastrous results when the abuser is out of control. Professional agencies need to assist the church in what to do. The last thing the church should do is kick the couple out!

One of the purposes of this devotional is to encourage CHURCHES to deal with domestic abuse. We have the Word of God. We have the Spirit of God. We have the presence of God. We have the Truth. There IS something the church can and should do to bring healing in very devastated relationships, and take steps that are SAFE.

Today my desire is to find a way to give the church a voice in confronting abuse in the home. This devotional guide is part of an educational process in learning what the scriptures say about domestic abuse, and learning safe ways to confront it. A plan for developing a ministry to the abused in the church is included in the Appendix of this devotional.

"The widow who is really in need
and left all alone
puts her hope in God
and continues night and day to pray and to ask
God for help."
(I Timothy 5:5)

III. ABUSE HURTS

Prayer Against Sin

Father of Mercy,
You have provided a way for my forgiveness.
Through Jesus You forgive me
with Your merciful heart.
I receive Your forgiveness and Your restoration.
As you have admonished us to also forgive others,
With Your strength right now, Lord,
I truly in my heart forgive my abuser
As he doesn't know what he is doing
And he is lost.
I will find my safe place away from him and his hurts
(as David did with Saul),
and leave all judgment and retribution into
Your hands.
He is yours, Oh Lord.
Convict him of his sin, and heal him.

"This is what the Lord says,
'Let not the wise man boast of his wisdom
Or the strong man boast of his strength

Or the rich man boast of his riches,
But let him who boasts boast about this:
That he understands and knows me,
That I am the LORD,
Who exercises kindness,
Justice and righteousness on earth,
For in these I delight.'" (Jeremiah 9:24)

I turn to You for the strength to stand up against sin,
sin directed at me, and sin directed at others.
I praise You for setting me free.
Amen.

Section IV

God Heals

I believe God
is the ultimate Healer—
of mind, body and spirit.

I believe Jesus
demonstrates God's power to heal.

I believe the Holy Spirit
can make me a "new creation."

IV. GOD HEALS

Day 25: Grieving the Loss

The loss hurts. It's the loss of a dream—from the beauty of a Bride's magazine to the ugliness of total division. The loss hurts, deep inside. Some of you reading this may still be with your partner, hopeful that things will get better. Maybe there have been some changes to make the environment a safer place for you. Or maybe you are separated from your partner, trying to survive alone. The grief process is taking hold, and you feel overwhelmed with some really tough realities.

The steps of grief are becoming real in your life.

Shock. It's as if you are hit on the head with a sledgehammer. The reality finally sets in that your marriage may be over. You may have tried numerous counseling settings, but things have become even more difficult at home. The day comes when you no longer feel SAFE with your partner. All you can think about is getting away. He threatens, he ignores, he punishes the dog, he holds all the money, he refuses to let you drive the car. Frankly, you are trapped and in his clutches, and every moment is fearful. You take a chance by talking to a professional abuse counselor by yourself, and the reality finally sets in. You feel no choice but to separate from him for your own safety.

Denial. At this point, playing the game of "denial" is finally over. You become honest with some supportive counselors, sharing the fearful environment at home. It seemed easier to put on blinders for years, pretending that the marriage was just fine. But the terror in the home has become too much. Throwing things, pounding the walls, threatening with a weapon, destroying possessions, slapping your face when you try to speak. The truth is finally coming out. It is an insecure time and an insecure place. Will he react with more devastating violence? Will he track you down to hurt you? Will he tell lies about you in the neighborhood or with other family members and friends? At this point it is vitally important for the victim to find assistance to live in a safe place to collect her thoughts. What are the chances of things quieting down? Will his anger subside? You have no assurance of this for your personal wellbeing. Actually true healing only comes when the truth is faced. Denial is over!

Anger. You want to respond with anger. You want to strike back, in overt or covert ways. The shock, denial and anger seem all wrapped up into one overwhelming emotion. Your world has suddenly been re-defined. A wife? A lover? All of this has seemed to profoundly change. Grief seems enormous, answers seem imperceptible, and your emotions are skewed beyond recognition.

Where is love, where is trust, where is peace? It's like your life needs to start all over. It's very clear what has happened. Your marriage covenant feels destroyed.

"But you have turned from the way
and by your teaching have caused many to stumble;
you have violated the covenant. . ."
(Malachi 2:8).

One of the biggest hurdles in the midst of all this turmoil is seeking the presence of God. You were joined together at the altar of the church in the sight of godly witnesses with vows of permanence, "'til death do us part." Now what?

God is so clear about his compassion for those who have gone astray in any area of life. He is there to be the Lover, the Counselor, the Deliverer, the Forgiver, the Restorer. He sees our faults, and He forgives us.

The Lord truly made them one in marriage. But He acknowledges that things can go wrong, seriously wrong, with this union. It is also clear that the Lord abhors the violence that has crept into a marriage.

> *"Has not the LORD made them one?*
> *In flesh and spirit they are his.*
> *And why one?*
> *Because he was seeking godly offspring.*
> *So guard yourself in your spirit,*
> *and do not break faith with the wife of your youth."*
> (Malachi 2:15)

The Lord also admonishes the husband to "guard yourself in your spirit" so that the marriage doesn't dissolve if he dares to break faith "with the wife of your youth."

> *"'I hate divorce,' says the Lord God of Israel,*
> *'and I hate a man's covering himself with violence*
> *as well as with his garment,' says the LORD Almighty.*

So guard yourself in your spirit, and
do not break faith."
(Malachi 2:16)

DO NOT BREAK FAITH WITH THE WIFE OF YOUR YOUTH! Several times in this chapter the Lord warns against breaking faith "with the wife of your youth." The harsh warning is given to the husband, as he is the one who is pivotal. The marriage can go this way, or that way, in his hands.

"It is because the LORD is acting as the witness
between you
and the wife of your youth,
because you have broken faith with her,
though she is your partner,
the wife of your marriage covenant."
(Malachi 2:14)

The Lord sees it all. He is the "witness." Marriage involves a "covenant" or a promise or a vow. And covenants are not to be broken recklessly. Put your anger aside and let the wrath of Almighty God deal with the sin. *"Do not repay anyone evil for evil...but leave room for God's wrath* (Romans 12:17,19b).

Acceptance. Finally, there is nothing more to do but accept the consequences of a broken relationship. There are some things that are not in your power to change. The Serenity Prayer gives us the wisdom that is needed:

"God, grant me the serenity to accept the things I cannot change,
The courage to change the things I can,
And the wisdom to know the difference."

Yes, God hates divorce. (He himself had to divorce Israel because of adultery/idolatry in Jeremiah 3:8.) So who doesn't hate divorce? In the context of this chapter, divorce may be the final result of violent assaults, which break the covenant. Divorce certainly is not the first step to take, but God has given it as a sad conclusion to a partnership that has failed due to violence. God really had a different plan for marriage. For divorce to be avoided, BOTH husband and wife need to humble themselves and seek help.

Grief takes hold. Grief sets in. Emotions plunge. But change must happen. Your life will take on a whole new direction once you insist that you will no longer accept abuse. You have been down to the depths of despair, but God has more for you. Once freed, you may find a whole new part of yourself that you never thought existed. You may find strength that you never knew you had. And you may finally find peace and rest. There IS a better way. Jesus said:

"Come unto me, all you who are weary and burdened,
and I will give you rest.
Take my yoke upon you and learn from me,
for I am gentle and humble in heart,
and you will find rest for your souls.
For my yoke is easy and my burden is light. . ."
(Matthew 11:28-30)

"May your fountain be blessed,
and may you rejoice in the wife of your youth."
(Proverbs 5:18)

IV. GOD HEALS

Day 26: Confessing Sins

The first step in finding healing from God is to look at our own sins. Have we sinned? The Bible is clear:

"For all have sinned and fall short of the glory of God."
(Romans 3:23)

"If we claim to be without sin, we deceive ourselves and the truth is not in us."
(I John 1:9)

". . .for no one living is righteous before you."
(Psalm 143:2)

And yet the victims of domestic abuse, and the sins against them are only too clear: being slapped, degraded, called names, etc. The truth is that an abuser who hurts a helpless victim IS committing sin against her. And the outcomes of persistent abuse will take its toll:

> *"The enemy pursues me,*
> *He crushes me to the ground;*
> *He makes me dwell in darkness*
> *Like those long dead.*
> *So my spirit grows faint within me;*
> *My heart within me is dismayed."*
> (Psalm 143:3-4)

The abuser doesn't realize that his intimidating actions and behaviors are really driving her away from him. He thinks he can FORCE the relationship, but that never works. Even though we may be in the category of the "abused," God wants us first to clean up our own hearts before we dwell on the sins of others. Is it apparent to you how you have sinned against God and against others? Have you listened to your own conscience? Have you made amends with those whom you have hurt? We MUST take this step in order to have a *"pure heart and a good conscience and a sincere faith"* (I Timothy 1:5). Jesus gives us this example:

"Why do you look at the speck of sawdust in
your brother's eye and pay no attention to the
plank in your own eye?"
(Matthew 7:3)

So we need to be honest with ourselves before God. Are there actions or words that have caused you to sin against your partner? How have you hurt him?

Let us confess our sins to God and receive His promised forgiveness. It may be a destructive habit, or a defect of character. It could be wrongs we have done, or hurts we have perpetrated on others. Whatever it is, tell God about it, receive his forgiveness, and then let that sin go! Forever! He has said he remembers our sins no more.

"You will again have compassion on us;
You will tread our sins underfoot
And hurl all our iniquities into the depths Of the sea."
(Micah 7:19)

Maybe it would help to write those sins on a piece of paper and then rip that paper to pieces before throwing it in the trash. After you have asked God's forgiveness, you may have to ask forgiveness from any others that you have hurt. You can do this in person or write a confession.

Almighty God forgives our sins because Jesus died on the cross in our place. He took the punishment for sins. We are free of condemnation because of Jesus! Visualize the word "FORGIVEN" written on your forehead.

Do you want someone to reciprocate and confess how he or she has hurt you? That is not part of this decision. We are just responsible for doing what God wants US to do. We have no control over what others will or will not do.

If we confess our sins to our abuser, how will it be received? Sadly, many abusers will use this confession to hurt you again. He may throw it back in your face, in effect saying, "I knew you were a failure." We cannot expect an abuser to understand or be willing to accept a sincere confession. My view is that we can confess how we have sinned against him, but we don't need to stay there and take another beating. If we want to make an attempt to confess our sins to our abuser, I think it is imperative that other people are present as witnesses, as well as referees if things suddenly escalate. This confession should be short and concise. And we are not in any way expecting the abuser to follow suit and confess his sins to you.

This is not a "trick" to get him to humbly confess his sins against you. In fact, most abusers are not able to sense that they are even hurting other people. They don't feel the empathy. You only confess your sins, or how you have hurt him, because that is what God wants you to fulfill. Nothing else. No manipulation.

I will share with you here that I made this step with my then husband. I felt convicted to ask his forgiveness for the mess our marriage was in. I went with some mutual friends of ours who drove me to his house. I confessed to him that I know I hurt him when I left him. I hurt him and his parents, and my parents, and our children, and our relatives, and our friends. I asked if he would forgive me.

Surprisingly to me, he got tears in his eyes, came over to me, and gave me a huge hug. He said softly, "I accept your apology. It wasn't all your fault." I responded that we could talk later. After praying with our friends, we tried to leave, and he walked me to the car with his arm around me. As I sat in the back seat, he knocked on the window and reached in to kiss me on the lips, saying he would get in touch with me. And we drove away. I was thoroughly praising God that I had this opportunity.

Did he get in touch with me? The answer is that this was the last contact I have had with him. No, he never responded. But I was not going there to expect a warm resolution of all our problems. I didn't expect him to even receive my apology. But he did voice that he received it, and that was the end of that.

Did he ask me to forgive him? No, but that is not what I was trying to induce. I want God to be his guide and the Holy Spirit to do the convicting.

After confessing our sins to God and to others, it is probably time to rest and retreat. We can rejoice in God's love for us, that he has truly forgiven and for-gotten our sins. Sit in quiet and just soak up His love.

Don't set up your expectations by thinking that others will reciprocate in their response to you as you confess your own sins. You are NOT doing this to receive anything from others. You are doing this simply out of obedience to God. Wait on Him to respond to you in an overflowing portion of His love:

> *"Let the morning bring me word of your*
> *Unfailing love,*
> *For I have put my trust in you.*

Show me the way I should go,
For to you I lift up my soul.
Rescue me from my enemies, O LORD,
For I hide myself in you.
Teach me to do your will,
For you are my God.
May your good Spirit
Lead me on level ground."
(Psalm 143:8-10)

"Show me the way I should go, for to you I lift up my soul." (Psalm 143:9)

IV. GOD HEALS

Day 27: Resolving Conflicts

Before we can find a clear conscience and a peaceful spirit, we must come to God and resolve conflicts HIS WAY. This means humbly taking responsibility for our own sins. How have we contributed to a conflict? Is your partner ALL WRONG? Or have you sinned against him as well? Our responsibility is ONLY to look at ourselves. We are not responsibility for what anyone else does, or doesn't do. They must answer to God as well as we do. We stand before God alone.

"Create in me a clean heart, oh God.
And renew a right spirit within me."
(Psalm 51:10)

That's our goal. *"Create in ME a clean heart."* We are only responsible for ourselves before God, and we have no control over anybody else.

Conflicts will always be part of the human condition. It started from the very beginning with Adam and Eve (Genesis 3) as well as their children, Cain and Abel (Genesis 4). Even the children of Israel had so many disputes that Moses had to appoint judges (Judges 2).

It was the beginning of the court system that we have today. I finally ended up in court, facing my husband and the judge for a solution to our difficulties. It was not easy. But I did feel protected by the court system, thanks to God.

But before court has to intervene, the Word of God does give us guidance on how to settle disputes, with a partner or with anybody. First we have to KNOW the steps, and then we have to do them. If your brother sins against you, the procedure stated in Matthew 18 is really very clear:

1. Go directly to the person with the conflict.
"If your brother sins against you, go and show him his fault, just between the two of you.
If he listens to you, you have won your brother over."
(Matthew 18:15)

2. Try to resolve it with two or three witnesses.

"But if he will not listen, take one or two others along,
so that every matter may be established
by the testimony of two or three witnesses."
(Matthew 18:16)

3. Tell it to the church.

"If he refuses to listen to them, tell it to the church;"
(Matthew 18:17)

4. Treat him as you would a pagan (or someone who is a lost sinner, not following God's ways).

"And if he refuses to listen even to the church, treat him
as you would a pagan or a tax collector."
(Matthew 18: 15-17)

That is supposed to work. But with the twisting of the abusive mind, sometimes it doesn't work. Sometimes a heated argument ensues if you even try to confront a difference in a peaceful way. Sometimes the stubbornness of the abuser makes him refuse to even try to reconcile. Sometimes sharing your feelings makes things worse. He makes you think that your ideas are crazy, and ends up pushing you off. When the anger level escalates to rage (out of control anger), it is a very dangerous time for a victim. The moment that signs of anger are escalating (loud voice, red face, slamming fists, throwing things, threatening words), she needs to retreat immediately. Get protection by involving someone else in the dispute.

Finding a witness also may be difficult because most abuse happens behind closed doors. An abuse counselor (and you have to search for them) is a rational choice to assist in reconciliation because they understand the dynamics that are in place. It's totally amazing how the profile of an abuser is extremely similar among men. They follow the same pattern, so counselors can recognize what is happening. Both partners need to humbly agree that seeing a counselor is an important step, admitting that the marriage is in jeopardy. The neutral counselor should give valued insight into the problems and have suggestions for the solution. If no progress is seen after six sessions, then the setting is not the right one. Each need to counsel separately.

If the abuser fails to agree to seek witnesses, then telling it to the church is next, although this too can become a challenge. Because we all usually appear at our polished best at church, the dysfunction may be hidden from others. No abuser blows up at church! This is also a risk because the leaders in the church may be in denial that abuse can ever be occurring in members of a Christian congregation. It may be too "embarrassing" for the elders of the church to bring it out for discussion. Remember, leaders in the church are generally not "professional abuse counselors." But God's Word should guide them. Their role is to LOVE both the abuser and the victim, and refer to professionals while supporting with Biblical principles.

If the victim has tried all these steps (going straight to the person, going with witnesses, going to the church) and there is no resolution of the problem, then the victim must find a place of safety for herself. In fact, the continued confrontations may make matters worse. It is imperative that the victim NEVER follows this order by herself. She is in a very weakened and vulnerable state. And if it is like my former husband, his biggest rage finally exploded when I opened up to the church. He also used the counseling office as a convenient place to blast me with all sorts of accusations. His spirit was not one wanting reconciliation, but only another place to fight.

When finally opening up to others about the destructive environment at home, I was totally amazed that some people just WOULD NOT BELIEVE IT. They didn't see it, and they don't believe it. Remember, the abuser is a charmer and he knows how to look good in public. Some people just can't believe that his personality changes at home. They don't WANT to believe it. It's just too much. I can't and don't base what I do on what OTHER PEOPLE think. I know the reality, and I stand on the truth. It's not up to me to convince them.

No progress can ever be made unless, out of humility, BOTH partners earnestly seek God, humbly desiring some help. Sometimes, circumstances FORCE an abuser to seek help. There may be a court order for anger management, or he may end up in jail. The crisis may finally bring him to face his defects, and do something about it. Or maybe she gives him an ultimatum. That's what I did. I said I wouldn't come back until we BOTH went to therapy. Sorry to say, my former husband made NO STEPS to seek professional counseling for himself. I don't know if he ever will. In his mind, this separation is all my fault.

God has given us pattern after pattern of HOW to live in peace:

"Get rid of all bitterness, rage and anger,
brawling and slander, along with every form of malice.
Be kind and compassionate to one another,
forgiving each other,
even as God for Christ's sake has forgiven you."
(Ephesians 4:31-32)

This passage alone, with no other, gives the path of life in our relationships.

My husband hangs on to bitterness, rage, anger, blame, slander and other forms of malice. All I want is for him to be kind and compassionate to me, and that both of us can forgive each other for our failings. But when you are in denial ("I didn't abuse her.") and are not willing to look within yourself to make some changes (blaming everybody and everything else for your troubles) , there really is no hope for healing.

If we think it is too hard to forgive someone who has wounded us, just remember that Jesus looked down from the cross, with nails in his hands and feet, and he said: *"Father, forgive them; for they don't know what they are doing"* (Luke 23:34). We need to forgive him in our hearts, but that doesn't mean that we put ourselves back in the same place. Any changes must be validated with DEEDS, not WORDS. One counselor told me that the separation should take at least one year so the new patterns can be established. Any lapse in that year (with some sort of violent behavior) cancels the whole arrangement.

"Dear children, let us not love with words or tongue but with actions and in truth."
(I John 3:8)

I agree. An abuser doesn't know what he is doing. He probably is very good with his words, which the scripture calls "smooth talk."

"His talk is smooth as butter, yet war is in his heart; his words are more soothing than oil, yet they are drawn swords."
(Psalm 55:21)

That's what has kept him floating for years. He knows how to charm with words, but the follow-up is non-existent. She believes him and gives him chance after chance after chance to make some real changes. But it doesn't happen! For this very reason, a victim needs to feel secure in a place of safety until there is an honest change. And that may take years of therapy.

Hurting a woman is a very deep psychological problem, and won't be fixed overnight.

"Be kind and compassionate to one another..."
(Ephesians 4:32)

IV. GOD HEALS

Day 28: Seeking Reconciliation

We all know the familiar words of the "Golden Rule":

"So in everything,
do to others what you would have them do to you,
for this sums up the law and the Prophets."
(Matthew 7:12)

We are urged to:

". . .live a life worthy of the calling you have received.
Be completely humble and gentle;
be patient, bearing with one another in love.
Make every effort to keep the unity of the Spirit
through the bond of peace."
(Ephesians 3:1-3)

Now THAT would be a peaceful life! The way God intended it. But in a dysfunctional relationship, this ideal never seems to come. You have tried to settle disputes directly with the abuser, but you never seem to resolve anything. You ask him to forgive you for your sins, but the environment doesn't change. The arguments continue, the threats soar, the intimidation worsens, the fear increases, and the lack of resolution only makes you feel completely frustrated. He is making you feel helpless and completely at his mercy. A momentary "sorry" comes again and again, but quickly seems to fade. Old patterns rear their ugly heads, only seeming to get worse with the passage of time.

Conflict is part of the human condition, and all of us need to learn how to resolve differences in a civil way. There are two different outcomes in a conflict. You might call it the "Path of Peace" or the "Path of Rage."

The Path of Peace

For most people the Path of Peace works. They learned it from their parents, their teachers, their acquaintances, their church. The big word is RESPECT for each other, and RESPECT for the opinions of others. When a conflict occurs, this is the path:

1. Recognize that you have a difference of opinion.
2. Listen to each other.
3. Determine how and why you have different viewpoints.
4. Discuss with each other to find a middle ground of agreement that you BOTH accept.
5. If step #4 doesn't readily happen, talk to some others who may have something to contribute from their experiences and wisdom.
6. Delay the decision and take time to pray.
7. Find a time when both parties are ready to resolve the differences in a mutually respectful way.

The key verse here is:

"Each of you should look not only to your own interest, but also to the interest of others."
(Philippians 2:4)

Notice that there is no name-calling, no threats, no demeaning words, no displays of physical anger, no hurts, no disrespect.

What happens in the Path of Rage?

The Path of Rage

1. Recognize you have a difference of opinion.
2. Voices get louder.
3. Faces become flushed with anger.
4. Body language becomes threatening (pounding on tables, etc.)
5. Remarks are made to degrade the other person (saying you are "stupid," etc.)
6. Objects are thrown across the room.
7. The dog is kicked.
8. Someone is prone to flee, and maybe does. The other wants to continue fighting, like slapping her across the face.
9. Physical assaults create injuries that need a doctor.
10. Someone calls 9-1-1 or the sheriff for protection.

The end result can vary at this point. First it can stop at any one place in this list by someone becoming subservient by giving up or saying "sorry." The strong person will usually get his way. Nothing is learned from this scenario. No real discussion took place. No respectful resolution was found. And the topic was "shoved under the rug."

The sad part is that the junk under the rug becomes bigger and bigger, and the risk of a final explosion is very predictable when it all comes out at once.

If he should make a vital decision, without her input, without respect for her views, and especially if it is done in secret, this would be considered a major act of abuse against her. It breaks the covenant of oneness with her.

What is Jesus' plan? We need to resolve personal or relational issues through **confession, repentance, reconciliation, restoration.**

If the couple comes to a decision that affects both of their lives, it is absolutely vital to learn safe ways to approach it. The Path of Peace works! But it takes learning some skills in resolving differences.

Sadly the dysfunctional relationship does everything the wrong way. One person powers over the other, and commits sinful acts of verbal, emotional and physical abuse. Before a dissension erupts into severe assaults, ONE OF THEM needs to stop. Refuse to discuss if tempers are out of control, and rage is taking over. Peace can only come when Jesus path of reconciliation is followed:

Confession.

"Therefore confess your sins to each other and pray for each other so that you may be healed. The prayer of a righteous man is powerful and effective."

(James 5:16)

Repentance.

"Repent, then, and turn to God,
so that your sins may be wiped out,
that times of refreshing may come from the Lord. . ."

(Acts 3:19)

Reconciliation.

"If your brother has something against you. . .
go and be reconciled."

(Matthew 18:15)

Restoration.

"But if we walk in the light, as he is in the light,
we have fellowship with one another,
and the blood of Jesus, his Son,
purifies us from all sin."

(I John 1:7)

Truly walking in the Light of Christ means we are different inside. We know we need forgiveness, and we are quick to forgive others (even abusers).

The secret to REALLY finding peace after a conflict is what Jesus has said in the verses above. He says we are "purified from all unrighteousness," and we are purified "from all sin." The very word "confess" should be equal to "repentance." We are SORRY for what we have done, and like the woman caught in adultery, Jesus says to us:

> "'Woman. . .Has no one condemned you?'
> 'No one sir,' she said.
> 'Then neither do I condemn you, ' Jesus declared.
> **'Go now and leave your life of sin** (emphasis mine).'"
> (John 8:10-11)

It's assumed that her behavior is altered and she will sin no more. There is a change! There is a turn-around. True repentance and confession mean we make a 180 degree turn.

So forgiveness with each other means there is a CHANGE. What happens with an abuser? He may refuse to give up his Path of Rage. It somehow makes him seem powerful. He really believes that SHE is the cause of his temper. He doesn't even see in himself how he is falling into a pattern of worsening rage and wrath. Again, it is a downward spiral, unless there is an intervention.

Sometimes it takes a catastrophic event to get his attention so that he will look at himself and what he has created in his marriage. Some men REFUSE to look at themselves, and REFUSE to reconcile, and never leave this life of rage.

But, she? She doesn't have to subject herself to his punishment. I have felt many times that all I wanted from my husband was an honest acceptance that things are a mess in our marriage, and that he would be willing to learn new ways in our relationship. Of course, this would mean humbling himself to admit he had been wrong, and kneeling at the foot of the cross to find forgiveness. That would be the start of reconciliation. I never saw it.

I believe that true reconciliation can come if the simple words of Jesus are followed:

Confess, repent, reconcile, restore. God can do that if we are willing. Statistics have shown that only 25% of abusers will finally come to the place of agreeing to make some changes. It can only start with his willingness to follow the new guidelines:

"For if you forgive men when they sin against you,
your heavenly Father will also forgive you.
But if you do not forgive men their sins,
our Father will not forgive your sins."
(Matthew 6:14-15)

IV. GOD HEALS

Day 29: Finding Restoration

Both the abuser and the victim within domestic abuse lead a life of confusion and turmoil. They have lived this way so long that they hardly know it can be anything different. The abusive patterns are entrenched, until finally one of them (usually the victim) says "No more!" Finding God's fullness of life is a complete turnaround. The pattern from scripture is this:

Confess. Admit you have sinned. Tell God you have sinned. Be specific and give no excuses (like, "I was tired," or "She irked me."). Acknowledge the hurt with honesty, realizing that this past sin may have some present consequences. Be truthful that you truly want to be forgiven by God and by others. Go to God with true confession. Then go to others and confess that you have sinned against them.

"Get rid of all bitterness, rage and anger,
brawling and slander, along with every form of malice.
Be kind and compassionate to one another,
forgiving each other, just as in Christ God forgave you."
(Ephesians 4:31-32)

Repent. As a result of this confession, you repent of this sin and seek to never let it return. You make a complete 180-degree turn, walking away from sinning again. And if a sin should creep in, you acknowledge this weakness and ask forgiveness immediately, from God and from others. The goal is keep a pure conscience before God.

"The goal of this command is love,
which comes from a pure heart and a good conscience
and a sincere faith."
(I Timothy 1:5)

Reconcile. There are probably areas that need to be specifically confronted. Differences of opinion happen in life. But differences do not mean that one person powers over the other to control the outcome. It is a learned skill to discern how conflicts are handled in a positive way. It is called Conflict Management, or God says it this way:

"'Come now, let us reason together,' says the Lord.
Though your sins are like scarlet, they shall be as
white as snow; though they are red as crimson they
shall be like wool.
If you are willing and obedient, you will eat the best
from the land; but if you resist and rebel, you will be
devoured by the sword.'
For the mouth of the Lord has spoken."
(Isaiah 1:18-20)

Notice in this scripture that being "willing and obedient" result in the best life has to offer. But if you "resist and rebel" you only in the end hurt yourself. Following God in obedience is the secret to a full and rich life, not only here but on into eternity.

It is important to NAME the sin if they are to be finally overcome. If it is "name-calling," resolve to stop. If it is "angry threats," resolve to keep threats out of the discussion. If it is punching or throwing things out of frustration, resolve to change this behavior. Overcoming angry outbursts is not an easy transition, and truly Anger Management Classes should help. Plus prayer! Soaking up God's Word daily DOES change your behavior as you see what it means to live in the light of Christ. Reconciling takes time, not an overnight process. But it is essentially important.

Restore. This step should be FUN! You have worked through the hard stuff of confession, repentance, and reconciliation. Your lives should become completely new. New ways of living and new ways of resolving differences. I have seen couples that have made the transformation to a new life in Christ and it is beautiful.

The last section of this book specifically speaks of ways to find this true restoration, whether your marriage is saved or whether it is dissolved. YOU need to be restored. Being restored with your partner is the very best outcome. But you may have to find restoration for yourself. It means returning to some sanity, returning to some peace, returning to a life without violence. God has intended for us to live in peace as we give our worries and anxieties to Him.

"Cast all your anxiety on him because he cares for you."
(I Peter 5:7)

God knows we are in a spiritual battle here on earth. Troubles will not cease, but how we react to them will make all the difference. Our enemy is Satan:

"Be self-controlled and alert.
Your enemy the devil prowls around like a roaring lion
looking for someone to devour.
Resist him, standing firm in the faith,
because you know that your brothers throughout the
world are undergoing the same kind of suffering.
And the God of all grace, who called you to his eternal
glory in Christ,
after you have suffered a little while,
*will himself **restore** you* (emphasis mine)
and make you strong, firm and steadfast.
To Him be the power for ever and ever. Amen."
(I Peter 5:8-14)

That's being restored: ***"strong, firm and steadfast."***
A very key element in finding restoration is turning to God, with our joys and with our sorrows. Praise Him in the joys, and praise Him in the sorrows because He is in charge. And when He is charge, there are no hurts that can't be overcome. Commit today to live every moment in His presence.

"Rejoice in the Lord always. I will say it again:
Rejoice!
Let your gentleness be evident to all.
The Lord is near.
Do not be anxious about anything,
but in everything, by prayer and petition,
with thanksgiving,
present your requests to God.
And the peace of God, which transcends
all understanding,
will guard your hearts and your minds
in Christ Jesus."
(Philippians 4:4-7)

Footnote: In my experience, my husband and I never got to step one, confession. I confessed how sorry I was that I hurt him when I left. He did not reciprocate. Without confession, nothing else resolves.

IV. GOD HEALS

Day 30: Letting It Go

One of the hardest things for a victim of abuse to do is to LET GO of her abuser. Does it sound strange that a victim hesitates to leave someone who is hurting her? There are many reasons why it is hard, but the main deterrent that keeps her in his clutches is FEAR. Fear of the unknown. She finds it easier to endure and keep the secret hidden than make any major changes. She doesn't want to "upset the apple cart" out of fear of what might happen next.

Once she makes a decision to come out of denial and start being honest about the treatment she has endured, she may finally find the strength to talk about her situation with a trusted friend or advisor. Once the lid comes off the box, she finds the freedom to keep talking. It is absolutely freeing to find a listening ear. Somebody is finally listening.

Unless the period of denial comes to an end, the situation will not only remain the same, but will also very possibly pivot downward into a deeper spiral of violence. It won't get "better with time." The elements of abuse are there, and their roots go deep in any relationship. Things always get worse, not better.

So first the victim needs to make a decision to put a stop to the sin of violence and abuse in her relationship. Before she makes a move, she needs a strong support group to give her stability. She has finally come to the point of believing and knowing that enduring the punishment of abuse is not God's will, and it's not healthy in a relationship. She makes plans to leave.

That's the start of "letting it go." She puts herself in a place that feels safe, and makes plans to STAY in a safe place. She separates herself from the abuse, maybe staying with her family or with friends, or at an abuse shelter for women. She can finally share what she has been going through, and she seeks advice from experts. The world will change for her, but it HAS to change. Above all, she needs to feel secure in a "safe place."

At this point what steps could be taken to save the marriage? Would he agree to meet with a counselor? Are there any signs of repentance? Has he crossed a legal line of assault so that charges need to be brought?

Are the problems "solvable"? The picture needs to be discussed with professionals who know the patterns.

After all outcomes have been researched, she makes one of two decisions:

1. Tell him she will stay with him if they both undergo therapy. Abuse counseling may take months, and even years, as our whole thinking patterns need adjustment.

2. She will decide that the marriage is showing no signs of being restored. He is fighting her even more in passive ways. (My husband, for example, withdrew all the money from the bank the morning after I left. He also changed all the locks in the house so that I could not get back in. He wanted to fight me still.)

The "letting go" means she has done all she knows how to do. He is not her responsibility anymore. He lives his life and she lives her life. He makes his decisions and she makes her decisions. She establishes her boundaries and sticks with them. If he contacts her, she has no responsibility to respond. She doesn't have to meet up with him. If he communicates with email or phone calls, she doesn't have to answer.

Does this sound stern? Well, the pattern of an abuser is to continue to hurt even after being separated. He has had every opportunity to show a change, and he will have to prove himself all over again if he hopes to save the relationship. She is DONE with the hurts, the deception, the manipulation, the malice.

She is ready to rebuild a new life with God as her guide! He will show her step by step what her life will now become.

One thing is sure. God's Word tells us numerous times to give our problems to Him. She is going to dwell in His peace and His rest.

"Come unto me, all you who are weary and burdened,
and I will give you rest.
Take my yoke upon you and learn from me
for I am gentle and humble in heart,
and you will find rest for your souls."
(Matthew 11:28-29)

I like to visualize wrapping up all my burdens in a package and dropping that package at the foot of the cross. I GIVE it to him. That means it is not my responsibility to handle all the turmoil in my life. God is there for me! He knows what I need, and He has promised to provide for me.

She may want to help her abuser, but the victim is probably the last person on earth to "help" him. She is actually a major trigger point to the abuser. The abuser not only rejects what she does or what she says, but he uses her every action to battle back against her. He has blind eyes and deaf ears to anything she has to say or do. She is the one who "sets him off." Why is that? Because she is the one—the only one—that he feels he can control. He certainly is not going to give her any credibility. He would rather feel the power he has over her than give in to her requests.

So she is not responsible to help him, and she really can't change him. An abuser has to decide to help HIMSELF. He has to come out of denial about his actions, recognizing that they are wrong. He has to seek help for himself on his own. Does this ever happen? Sorry to say that it is a rare abuser who finds healing for himself and seeks a change. His torments have deep psychological roots, and only a professional therapist can bring him to health and freedom.

So she needs to LET GO of him. My letting go meant that I didn't need him for anything—not money, not housing, not possessions, not a car. That was the last hold he had on me, thinking I would come back to him for some basic needs. No, I was finally out of his clutches.

We also need to let go of retaliation. Having a vindictive response to hurts is a natural (worldly) response. But God has told us a new way. He says that it is HIS job to deal with sin. We are not to return evil for evil. We are not to strike back.

> *"Bless those who persecute you;*
> *bless and do not curse. . . .*
> *Live in harmony with one another. . . .*
> *Do not repay anyone evil for evil.*
> *Be careful to do what is right in the eyes of everybody.*
> *If it is possible, as far as it depends on you,*
> *live at peace with everyone.*
> *Do not take revenge, my friends,*
> *but leave room for God's wrath, for it is written:*
> *'It is mine to avenge; I will repay,' says the Lord.*
> *On the contrary: 'If your enemy is hungry, feed him;*
> *if he is thirsty, give him something to drink.*
> *In doing this, you will heap burning coals on his head.'*
> *Do not be overcome by evil, but overcome evil*
> *with good."*

(Romans 12:14; 16-21)

"Letting go" means not trying to "change" an abuser.

"Letting go" means giving it to God to resolve.

"Letting go" means not striking back.

"Letting go" means God is responsible for judging and punishing sin.

"Letting go" means we will respond with love and prayer for the abuser.

"*...overcome evil with good.*" (Romans 12:21)

IV. GOD HEALS

Day 31: Forgiving and Forgetting

It's an easy slogan to say, "forgive and forget." The forgiving part may seem easier, while the forgetting part seems impossible. Actually I have people say to me, "Why don't you just forgive and forget?" Why? Because nothing changed in the relationship. Nothing! I felt like I was standing on the edge of cliff, ready to forgive and forget, and start anew with him. But I got NO indication that he was willing to work out our differences.

An essential element in REALLY forgiving someone is to DROP THE SUBJECT.

We say before God and before another that we "forgive them," even though their deeds are dastardly. In fact, Jesus encouraged us to forgive "seventy times seven".

"Then Peter came to Jesus and asked,
'Lord, how many times shall I forgive my brother
when he sins against me? Up to seven times?'
Jesus answered, 'I tell you, not seven times,
but seventy times seven.'"
(Matthew 18:21-22)

Jesus follows this statement with an example of a servant who was forgiven of his debts by his master, but then refused to forgive a fellow servant who owed him money. Since the servant showed no mercy to his debtor, the master required that he pay back his original debt. And beyond that, the master *"turned him over to the jailers to be tortured, until he should pay back all he owed"* (Matthew18:34). That's a harsh response! But the point is strongly made that we are to forgive others just as we are forgiven:

"This is how my heavenly Father will treat each of you
unless you forgive your brother from your heart."
(Matthew 18:35)

If and when a past negative event comes to my mind, I strongly put a seal over my mouth and do not tell the story out loud. And then I need to quickly change my thoughts over to something else that is positive. Truthfully, I used to share stories all the time, in an effort for someone to understand me. Now those stories belong only to the confidence of counselors. Sometimes sharing stories flippantly can come back to hurt you again. Sometimes it's the start of slander and gossip. It accomplishes nothing.

The *Peacemaker Ministry* names "Four Promises of Forgiveness," or four reminders to assure us that we have truly forgiven someone else "from your heart:"

1. I will not dwell on this incident.
2. I will not bring this incident up and use it against you.
3. I will not talk to others about this incident.
4. I will not allow this incident to stand between us or hinder our personal relationship.

It requires an intentional effort to stop letting our thoughts be consumed with hurtful memories and replace them with positive thoughts to fill the void. We have no need to repeat and repeat all the ways we have been hurt. Those days are GONE. Starting each day with a fresh spirit of forgiveness is now our new *modus operandi*, or our NEW way of thinking. We pray for God's help in keeping our thoughts pleasing to him.

Ask yourself the question: Does it make you feel better to dwell on the abusive acts you endured, or would you feel better simply by putting them behind you? Dwelling on the abuse only intensifies the struggle to overcome it. It's like the abuser still owns your thoughts, to torment you. It will take a concerted effort, with God's strength, to overcome the fact that abuse seems to saturate your mind. Look at yourself as a "new creature" before God:

"Therefore, if anyone is in Christ, he is a new creation; the old has gone, the new has come."
(2 Corinthians 5:17)

THE OLD HAS GONE!

There are several steps to cross before you can fully feel like you are a "new creation" and the "old has gone."

- You make the decision that you will not live under an abusive environment any longer.
- You seek a support system (professional and spiritual) so that you can stay in a "safe place."
- You look for God's purposes in your life with each new day.

- You surround yourself with God's Word so that your thoughts and behaviors can be controlled by his Holy Spirit.
- You prayerfully wait on the Lord to fulfill His purposes in your life.
- You willingly accept and embrace positive changes that occur in your life.
- You look FORWARD!

Keep in mind that it is NEVER in God's will for anyone to be hurt over and over again. You are keeping a clear conscience before God. You cannot control what anyone else will or will not do, but you will be committed to doing what is right in God's eyes:

"Take your evil deeds
Out of my sight!
Stop doing wrong,
Learn to do right!
Seek justice,
Rebuke the oppressor.
Defend the cause of the fatherless,
Plead the case of the widow."
(Isaiah 1:16-17)

"Take your evil deeds out of my sight." That means you are done with the sin of abuse.

"Stop doing wrong, learn to do right." That is directed toward your abuser. You are calling his abuse "wrong," and admonishing him to "do right."

"Seek justice." That means that justice will eventually be accomplished.

It may seem like "justice" if he is jailed for assault, or ordered by the court to attend Anger Management classes. But neither of these events provide true "justice." God sees it all, and He is the ultimate Judge, Jury and Executioner. "Justice" is in His hands, and that can't get any better. Additionally, the victim may never feel justice was done. What consequences did he incur for being an abuser? I say, don't even think about it! God will take care of the justice. Now you are free from the abusive environment. Be thankful to God, and move on with your own life.

"Rebuke the oppressor." That means you FINALLY stood up to the abuse. You exposed the sin. The abuse is now public, and that is his "rebuke." You did your job by not keeping the big "secret" hidden anymore. He is rebuked!

"Defend the cause of the fatherless, plead the case of the widow." That means you will focus your life

on how to serve others. You are no longer burdened with trying to get through each day with the continual battles of abuse. You are free to do what God wants you to do.

God has given you a new place:

"One thing I do:

Forgetting what is behind and straining

toward what is ahead,

I press on toward the goal to win the prize for which

God has called me heavenward in Christ Jesus."

(Philippians 3:13b-14)

When those negative memories start to flood your mind again, intentionally say, "STOP." Force yourself to focus on something else. Quote a Bible verse to yourself, or sing a praise song. Refuse to let your mind become entangled in past memories. It does no good!

In place of the negative past in your life, think about these things, with God's help:

"Finally, brothers, whatever is true, whatever is noble,

whatever is right, whatever is pure,

whatever is lovely, whatever is admirable—

if anything is excellent or praiseworthy—

think about such things.

*Whatever you have learned or received or
heard from me,
or seen in me—put it into practice.
And the God of peace will be with you."*
(Philippians 4:8-9)

"...forgetting what is behind..." (Philippians 3:13b)

IV. GOD HEALS

Day 32: Staying Honest

Abusers live in a world of deception. Their "real self" comes out behind closed doors. They are one person in public, and a totally different world in private. This dual personality demonstrates that their core is damaged, and some things are missing in their inner self:

- They can't maintain deep relationships.
- They are extremely private people, feeling the best when they are alone.
- They resist going out with friends, including times "with the guys." (I think it is because they can't be with people too long because it's too hard to keep up the false front.)
- They are very good at presenting a "pseudo" or false self in social situations for a short period of time.

- They will do everything in their power to keep the "secret."
- They find a partner (someone usually weaker in their persona) for their own needs, not her needs.
- They will find it easy to exaggerate or outright lie to preserve this persona.
- Unable to face things themselves, they will easily blame someone else for their problems. They are NEVER at fault.
- They find it difficult, if not impossible, to be truthful about their feelings. In fact, maybe they don't really "feel" that they are hurtful in their behaviors.
- They CAN'T tell the truth.

Basically, abusers live in a world of deception. They cannot be HONEST, with themselves or with others.

If and when an abuser's partner starts to question some things in their lives, he is not willing or able to discuss it. He will either snap back with a quick retort, or get in the car and drive away, or attack her with verbal put downs. Sometimes it's a slap across the face to keep her quiet. It makes her feel "wrong" as he was able to shut her up.

But the day may come when she matures to the point of realizing that things in their lives are not what they should be. She is shut down when she tries to express her feelings. He seems to be getting angrier and angrier with every argument. With his deepening anger, she is becoming more afraid of him and what he might do. SHE is the one who finally faces the situation with HONESTY.

It is true that the "truth shall set you free." Jesus is the One who said it:

"If you hold to my teaching, you are really my disciples.
Then you will know the truth, and the truth
will set you free."
(John 8:31-32)

When the truth starts to come out, Pandora's box is opened, and the garbage is revealed. Speaking TRUTH is the beginning of the end of the dysfunction. It's called "coming out of denial."

If TRUTH is what breaks the cycle of violence, then the opposite is also true. Deception maintains the violence, and secrets prolong the suffering. It is absolutely required by an abuser to keep things SECRET. A violent event, ending in either bloodshed or a trip to the

ER, is not to be revealed in public. The victim may go to extreme ends to cover up such assaults, and is really good at making excuses for her abuser. In public the couple certainly doesn't have the look of dysfunction. In fact, they both know how to dress it up so that the secret remains hidden. Outwardly they look just fine.

Another problem for the victim is that she may want to avoid consequences that could come her way if she dares to say a word to anyone. She may be criticized as being "crazy" or "emotionally maladjusted" or "unstable." The abuser is very good at telling others how deficient and inept she is.

(One of my husband's biggest lies was to tell people that I "ran off with another woman" when I finally left the house.)

Then a day comes when the TRUTH comes out in bold letters in her mind. **THIS IS DOMESTIC ABUSE.** It was very difficult for me to face the truth of those words. For me it was in the doctor's office when I was asked if I feel "safe" at home. I read a chart on the wall that described the elements of an abusive relationship. It was US. I finally became convinced that I had to make a change. I was feeling downtrodden and defeated and helpless, and I wanted it to stop.

If the victim goes for help, her partner may realize that their relationship is in deep jeopardy. Maybe, just maybe, he will agree to find help as well. But most of the time, it is the victim that reaches out for help, and the abuser is not at all ready to comply. Some men do a minimum or a token act of trying to repair the relationship. In public, it LOOKS like he is sincerely seeking a change. He starts to make some promises how things will be better.

Many women at this point quickly go back. After all, "He promised." But without any real intention of making a change, the abuser has successfully manipulated the victim back into his grip. He may agree to go to some marriage counseling (and I can testify that the counseling office only becomes another place for him to batter you in front of others.). He thinks it will ease the pressure for himself for the time being if he goes to a few counseling sessions, but then he goes right back to his old ways when she is weak or vulnerable again. It is difficult for him to admit that he might have an "anger management" problem. And there really is no "quick fix."

I went to a few sessions of joint counseling with high hopes. I thought, "He wants to make some changes. Hallelujah! Things will get better." Sadly, in the counselor's office the lies and blame and accusing only intensified. He had the nerve to use that setting as another battleground to attack me as a person. It didn't work. And it won't work unless both come with a pure heart of wanting to repent and make some changes to save the marriage.

The victim has every right in the world to protect herself. She puts up her boundary of not being the victim of verbal or physical or emotional assaults. Unless he learns how to treat her with mutual respect, the relationship is over. She faces the TRUTH.

This is called BEING HONEST! She is finally coming out of denial and facing the fact that she is in a very destructive marriage. The abuse hurts her and it hurts him as well since both of their lives are in chaos. The dysfunction may show in money problems, drinking problems, job problems, depression problems. The chaotic life of an abuser is out of control in numerous places. As the years go by, the problems intensify and finally there may be an explosion of some sort, which brings the boil to a head. No more is it possible to live the "pseudo life" in front of others.

It usually is HONESTY that becomes the trigger for another explosion at home:

"You didn't pay the mortgage."
"You just kicked the dog."
"You just lied to your boss."
"You took some of my money."
"You just pushed me."
"You came home drunk last night."
"You just threw chairs across the room."
"You are overdrawn at the bank."

He can't bear the honesty! The truth is coming out! The more honesty she speaks, the more agitated he becames.

Jesus calls us to do what is right, even though the consequences may be difficult. He says not to "*grow weary and lose heart.*"

"*Let us fix our eyes on Jesus,*
      the author and perfecter of our faith,
   who for the joy set before him endured the cross,
 scorning its shame, and sat down at the right hand of
               the throne of God.
     Consider him who endured such opposition
               from sinful men,
   so that you will not grow weary and lose heart."
(Hebrews 12:2-3)

Jesus calls us to persevere in the midst of suffering. There is suffering in staying, and there is also momentary suffering in leaving. But the dangers of wrath and rage in domestic abuse are so intense, that a victim CANNOT stay in that place anymore. It is NOT SAFE. God will need to show her a new way, and He will. Stay committed to living a pure and honest life before God and man.

BE HONEST! To yourself, to others, and to God!

When someone degrades you.
When someone humiliates you.
When someone hits you.
When someone calls you names.
When someone ignores you
When someone takes your stuff,
When someone abandons you.
When someone does "all evil against you."

Call it what it is! Name it out loud. THOSE DAYS ARE OVER! There will be no more secrets. You will put up your hand, stand your ground, and say, "STOP"! You will respond with honesty about how someone has hurt you. You will wait for reconciliation. If he agrees to get some help, then the relationship should and could improve. If he does not agree, then you will walk away. You don't have to live with this! Pull alongside others who know what it means to live with mutual respect, and learn what a healthy relationship is all about. Do not grow weary or lose heart. Strive with all your heart to do what is RIGHT.

Stay honest! Stay truthful! Express your feelings! Commit to doing what it right! Refuse to stay in the darkness.

And don't be surprised if your abuser doesn't understand a thing you are saying. The thinking patterns of an abuser are in a totally different realm. He cannot see his own sin. He refuses to examine his heart out of insecurity. It is easier to continually put up a false front with others. He has a lifetime pattern of deceiving others, and actually lying to himself. He cannot admit his sin. He is just simply too blind to find a place of honesty.

But that will not discourage you. It is the job of the Holy Spirit to convict of sin, not yours. You can express yourself, but understand that he is at a different place inside his dark cave. He will not come out into the light. He cannot be honest. That's when he tries to hurt you in some way, when you speak with honesty. Somehow staying in his cave by himself, and creating a false image with lies and deception, is the only place he knows how to survive. His lack of any self-esteem means he CAN'T tell the truth because he feels like a failure. You WERE the one thing in his life that he could feel powerful over, and now you are confronting him with truth. It's too much for him. And truthfully, it requires deep psychological therapy to overcome a life of abusing others. The root of this abusive pattern goes way back to childhood.

For you? Protect yourself. Become the person God wants you to be in all freedom. Stay away from the darkness, and stay in the light of truth.

"The path of the righteous is like the first
Gleam of dawn,
Shining ever brighter till the full light of day.
But the way of the wicked is like
Deep darkness.
They do not know what makes them stumble.
My son, pay attention to what I say;
Listen closely to my words.
Do not let them out of your sight,
Keep them within your heart;
For they are life to those who find them
And health to a man's whole body.

"Above all else, guard your heart, for it is the wellspring of life."
(Proverbs 4:18-23)

IV. GOD HEALS

Prayer for God's Healing

Father of Restoration, healing is in Your wings.
With the touch of Your garment,
Healing rushes out of You in mighty power.

Father, we learn deep lessons through suffering.
Most of all, we learn that You are right there with us.
You bring wholeness when all else is crumbling.
You have said, *"all things work together for good"*
(Romans 8:28)
And we believe that.

You are there to heal our bodies, our souls, and our
spirits.
You perform mighty deeds through us
And it all brings glory back to You.
Relying on You is the safest place for us.
You are there!
You are there!
You are there!
Father, I long to live in your Truth,
For you are *"the way, the truth and the life."*
(John14:6)
Lead me, guide me, and heal me—completely!

Amen

Section V

God Restores

I believe God
forgives me of my sins.

I believe God
empowers me to forgive others
as I have been forgiven.

I believe God
can "renew my mind"
so I can live my life
according to His divine purposes.

V. GOD RESTORES

Day 33: Finding Acceptance

This is the last step! Acceptance is our goal! It may be a long journey of healing and working through each of the steps of faith:

- God made me.
- God loves me.
- Abuse hurts.
- God heals me.
- God restores me.

Final acceptance is a vital step in total healing. I may not like this lot in life that I have had to endure. It has only been to easy to whisper, "Why me?" But there are some things that we cannot change, and must simple accept. When God is in the picture, He can use the whole circumstance for His honor and glory.

Most victims of abuse can hardly say it out loud: "I was a victim of domestic abuse." Maybe it would be easier to say: "I am a survivor of domestic abuse." It certainly gets people's attention, and you are just speaking the truth. But the Truth is what sets you free. No more pretending!

"If you hold to my teaching, you are really my disciples.
Then you will know the truth,
and the truth will set you free."
(John 8:31-32)

There are times when conversing with people that I am able to share, "I am a survivor of domestic abuse." It opens up meaningful conversations. Often women feel free to share their personal stories with me. When I get honest with others, they get honest as well, and feel free to open up and share the abuse they have been in. I take this "mission" very seriously. If a woman opens up to me about abuse in her life, it starts on-going conversations on the phone or on email. My goal is to give them insight, encouragement and support to do the right thing.

It's not easy to open up. There are elements in an abusively dysfunctional relationship that may hold a victim back from standing against her abuser. She really DOES feel love in her heart for him. She doesn't know why their relationship changed. She trusted him with her life, but now the trust is gone. She put up with the pattern of abuse for so many years that she can hardly imagine how things could be different. She is aware of her friends, as some will stand by her and others will shun her. How would the church ever understand? How will this affect the children, and extended family members? Inside, she may feel confusion about what to do. Basically she may feel SHAME that she is caught in such a mess. It feels like extreme weakness.

But inside her heart she knows the TRUTH. She knows that doing nothing only enables an abuser to continue his destructive paths. She looks to the future with doubt and insecurity, but then she knows she MUST take the risk in order to make a change. The end result of domestic abuse is destruction and it could be fatal. Most "murder/suicide" happenings are the end result of complete dysfunction in the home. The insecurity about what will happen next can be paralyzing.

Being obedient to Jesus' teaching should be the driving force of our decisions. Jesus said, *"If you hold*

to my teaching, you are really my disciples" (John 8:31).
Obedience! Standing up to sin is part of Jesus' teaching.

Keep Jesus' teachings clear in your mind and heart as He is the motivation for how we live. Here are a few concise examples from Ephesians that show us life with Christ:

TRUTH
"Therefore each of you must put off falsehood and speak truthfully to his neighbor. .

ANGER
In your anger do not sin.
Do not let the sun go down while you are still angry. . .

DEVIL
Do not give the devil a foothold

STEALING
He who has been stealing must steal no longer,

WORK
but must work, doing something useful with his own hands, that he may have something to share with those in need.

TALK

Do not let any unwholesome talk come out of your mouths, but only what is helpful for building others up according to their need.

GRIEVING THE SPIRIT

Do not grieve the Holy Spirit of God.

BITTERNESS

Get rid of all bitterness,

RAGE

rage and anger,

SLANDER

brawling and slander

MALICE

along with every form of malice.

KINDNESS

Be kind and compassionate to one another,

FORGIVENESS

forgiving each other, just as in Christ God forgave you.

LOVE

Be imitators of God, therefore, as dearly loved children
and live a life of love, just as Christ loved us
and gave himself up for us
as a fragrant offering and sacrifice to God."
(Ephesians 4:23–5:2)

This is only one passage in Scripture, but there are many others that help us know how to live in peace with Christ at the center. Anybody reading this one list will conclude that this is surely God's idea of a healthy relationship between husband and wife as well as ALL other relationships. Abuse is the dire opposite of this list.

It may take some education (as it did with me), but finally and hopefully a victim will come to the point of truthfully accepting what has happened to her, making a decision to bring it to a stop, and looking to a new future with God's guidance.

Acceptance finally comes. You have accepted what you cannot change. The secret is finally out, and the truth is this: you are a survivor of domestic abuse. Accept it! Is God done with you? Maybe He is just beginning to work in your life in a bigger way. He may have something more for you, something that you never could have predicted. But be assured that He is not done with you yet!

"I thank my God every time I remember you.
In all my prayers for all of you,
I always pray with joy because of your partnership in
the gospel
from the first day until now, being confident of
this, that

He who began a good work in you will
carry it on to completion until the day of
Christ Jesus."
(Philippians 1:3-6).

V. GOD RESTORES

Day 34: Moving Forward

People may say, "Just move on with your life." Well, that is not so easy to do. You have invested years, maybe decades, trying to bring stability and rationality to a close relationship. And it doesn't seem to go anywhere. Nothing seems to change. In fact, things seem to be deteriorating with time. When you take a little step forward to initiate a change, it may not only be rejected, but may be thrown back in your face as "foolish" or "ignorant." (Those are words my husband threw at me.) An abuser will not take suggestions from his victim. He sees it as a source of weakness.

Victims of abuse need to recognize their limits. It is not our responsibility to "change" someone. In fact, that is an impossibility. God is the only One, through his Holy Spirit, who can reach into a person's heart.

And that's where change has to start. You have to get to the source.

> *"Make a tree good and its fruit will be good,*
> *or make a tree bad and its fruit will be bad,*
> *for a tree is recognized by its fruit."*
> (Matthew 12:33)

So we recognize that the fruit of the abuser is behavior that is not pleasing to God. That means it is "sin." And where does this sin come from?

> *"You brood of vipers, how can you who are evil say any-*
> *thing good?*
> *For out of the overflow of the heart the mouth speaks.*
> *The good man brings good things out of the good*
> *stored up in him,*
> *and the evil man brings evil things*
> *out of the evil stored up in him."*
> (Matthew 12:34-35)

The evil comes from inside the heart!

God is not only aware of this sin, but it is His responsibility to deal with it. He is the ONLY ONE through His Holy Spirit who can bring a "heart change."

The end result is that the abuser (like everyone else) will someday have to give account for his actions to Almighty God.

"I tell you that men will have to give account
on the day of judgment for every careless word they
have spoken.
For by your words you will be acquitted,
and by your words you will be condemned."
(Matthew 12: 36-37)

That's why we let it go. God WILL take care of it.

The difference between an "evil" person and a "good" person is the attitude of the heart. The "good" person has felt the conviction of the Holy Spirit and humbly falls on his or her knees, asking forgiveness from God. The "evil" person does not listen to the conviction of the Holy Spirit, but holds on to his or her pride, refusing to admit that he or she is a "sinner" in need of a Savior. An "evil" person will blame others for every malady, not taking responsibility for his or her own behaviors. A "good" person acknowledges the sin in his or her life, and quickly responds to the prodding of the Holy Spirit to repent of sin.

Do "good" people ever do wrong? Do "evil" people ever do right? Of course, both do. If we feel the need to understand "why," that question may never be answered. We only see the outside, but God sees the heart. We may never know the deep reasons why an abuser is an abuser. All we do know is that we will never more become the brunt of an abuser's torments. And he is tormented.

There are many factors that cause a person to do wrong. The problems arise from deep inside the psyche, which is why they are so difficult to fix. It could be a personality disorder, narcissism, character flaws, desperation, fear, learnt behaviors, arrested development. Only an educated psychotherapist has the tools to dig out the root causes of evil impulses. It certainly has a spiritual root as well, with the root of the evil going back to the reality of Satan Himself.

"Be self-controlled and alert.
Your enemy the devil prowls around like a roaring lion
looking for someone to devour.
Resist him, standing firm in the faith,
because you know that your brothers throughout the
world are undergoing the same kind of suffering."
(I Peter 5:8-9)

We are not helpless victims of the evil in the world. The Lord God has the power to overcome these evil intents.

"And the God of all grace, who called you to his eternal glory in Christ, after you have suffered a little while, will himself restore you and make you strong, firm and steadfast.
To him be the power for ever and ever. Amen."
(I Peter 5:10-11)

The Word of God tells us clearly that we are in a spiritual battle here on earth:

"For our struggle is not against flesh and blood, but against the rulers, against the authorities, against the powers of this dark world and against the spiritual forces of evil in the heavenly realms."
(Ephesians 5:12)

So there is an evil force battling for souls in this world. At the same time, God gives us every protection against the assaults of evil. He says to put on His armor:

"Therefore put on the full armor of God,
so that when the day of evil comes,
you may be able to stand your ground,
and after you have done everything to stand."
(Ephesians 5:13)

From these verses, we can see that God wants us to move forward with strength—"*strong, firm and stead-fast*" despite the evil in the world. He says to "*stand your ground*" against the evil. That's what we must do with the evil of domestic abuse.

We may spend many hours trying to figure out the "why" of domestic abuse, but the answer may never come. It's time to let that search go!

That is the only way to ever really "move on" in this relationship. Actually, it may never completely go away. The scars will always remain. And they affect who we are today. Maybe we live more carefully, locking doors, always knowing where our car keys are, keeping our phone charged. Is that living in fear? No, it is taking personal responsibility for our safety.

And we know our boundaries. We will NOT endure degrading treatment by others. We will seek to find strength, with God's help, to live in His righteousness. We will not be easy prey for a violent man. We will stand strong, and stay away unless and until a professional abuse counselor can help to bring the relationship out of dysfunction and into health. We will stay accountable to a strong group of supporters, either friends and family, or professional counselors. And most important of all, we will stay close to God by devouring his Word and praying.

If you have done everything within your power to resolve conflict, you have fulfilled your responsibility toward God and may STOP actively trying to solve the problem. If circumstances change, with new opportunities to seek peace with your opponent, you can give it a try (after much counsel and never alone with the abuser). The reality is that it is not necessary or wise to waste time, energy, and resources fretting over someone who refuses to be reconciled. In fact, the scripture says to LET HIM GO:

"But if the unbeliever leaves, let him do so.
A believing man or woman is not bound
in such circumstances; God has called us to live in
peace."
(I Corinthians 7:15)

Am I making a judgment call on whether someone is a believer or not? I just say, "I don't know." But Jesus gives us some insight when He said to look at the fruits:

"By their fruit you will recognize them.
Do people pick grapes from thornbushes, or figs from
thistles?
Likewise every good tree bears good fruits,
but a bad tree bears bad fruit.
A good tree cannot bear bad fruit, and a bad tree
cannot bear good fruit.
Every tree that does not bear good fruit is cut down
and thrown into the fire.
Thus, by their fruit you will recognize them."
(Matthew 7:16-20)

That imagery speaks to me: "grapes from thorn-bushes" or "figs from thistles." It's a clear picture that the fruits of a person's life show their heart and their closeness to walking with God. That's as far as I will go. I just look at the fruit, and guard my heart.

So we give our minds and our hearts a REST. We will not dwell on the past, or let our thoughts stagnate by reviewing things over and over in our minds. No longer will our abuser have control over our thoughts.

We are moving FORWARD! Fear is replaced with faith. Worry is replaced with trust. Anger is replaced with peace. Stagnation is replaced with purpose. Despair is replaced with hope. Isolation is replaced with the unfailing love of God.

Out of the depths I cry to you, O LORD;
O Lord, hear my voice.
Let your ears be attentive to my cry for mercy.
If you, O LORD, kept a record of sins,
O Lord, who could stand?
But with you there is forgiveness;
Therefore you are feared.
I wait for the LORD, my soul waits,
And in his word I put my hope.
My soul waits for the Lord,
More than watchmen wait for the morning.
O Israel, put your hope in the LORD,
For with the LORD is unfailing love
And with him is full redemption. (Psalm 130)

"I wait for the LORD, my soul waits..."
(Psalm 130:5).

V. GOD RESTORES
Day 35: Accepting Suffering

So suffering will always be part of my life? Nobody ever promises that there comes a point in life where there is no more suffering. In fact, it is the moments of suffering that we find ourselves in a position of either becoming "bitter or better." The suffering can leave us with a hardened heart, unyielding, bitter, resentful, vindictive; or it can be the source of positive growth as a person. It forces us to look inward, if we are willing to examine ourselves on a deeper level. How does this suffering build character? God says, "It will!"

"And we rejoice in the hope of the glory of God.
Not only so, but we also rejoice in our sufferings,
because we know that suffering produces perseverance;
perseverance, character; and character, hope.
And hope does not disappoint us,

because God has poured out his love
in our hearts by the Holy Spirit, whom he has given us."
(Romans 4:4-5)

Rejoice in our sufferings. That's what it says, because the suffering eventually brings us to a new and better place. We become more trusting and more intimate with God as we turn to Him for deeper meaning in our lives. Trusting Him brings a stronger faith, which is "greater than gold."

"In this you greatly rejoice, though now for a little while
you may have had to suffer grief in all kinds of trials.
These have come so that your faith—of greater worth
than gold, which perishes even though refined by
fire—may be proved genuine and may result in praise,
glory and honor when Jesus Christ is revealed."
(I Peter 1:6-7)

We turn to Christ with all our hearts and all our souls and all our strength. And the end result is joy that is beyond words:

"Though you have not seen him, you love him;
and even though you do not see him now,

you believe in him and are filled with an inexpressible
and glorious joy,
for you are receiving the goal of your faith,
the salvation of your souls."
(I Peter 1:8-9)

Filled with an "inexpressible and glorious joy." That sounds like the top of the mountain to me. Somehow our sufferings purify us, or burn away all the impurities, leaving only solid gold. In the end it is the suffering that molds our lives to genuine character.

Of course, we need to stay in close touch with God, being honest about how the sufferings are affecting us. Remember how Moses fought for the release of the suffering children of Israel while they were in slavery in Egypt. They suffered for over 400 years, but their "savior" in Moses finally came and God set them free. The time had to be right. During their captivity, most of them held on to their faith in the midst of decades of suffering. Imagine their joy when they were finally set free, by the miraculous hand of God. God said to "remember Egypt" (Deuteronomy 5:15) and how he rescued them out of a devastating situation (Exodus 5-12).

"By faith Moses. . .chose to be mistreated along with
the people of God
rather than to enjoy the pleasure of sin
for a short time.
He regarded disgrace for the sake of Christ
as of greater value than the treasures of Egypt,
because he was looking ahead to his reward.
By faith he left Egypt, not fearing the king's anger;
he persevered because he saw him who is invisible."
(Hebrews 11:24–27)

Moses had a choice. He could have stayed in the comforts of Egypt in the house of the Pharaoh. But he chose to be faithful to his calling as a Hebrew himself. As God spoke to him in the burning bush (Exodus 3), he freely gave his life to free the Hebrew slaves. Did this happen overnight? No, it took years for Moses to find complete obedience to God.

The huge lesson here is that God—"him who is invisible"—has the big picture. We have limited vision and only see "through a glass darkly" (I Corinthians 13). The day will come when we will see clearly what God is doing in our lives. Right now we live by FAITH. Faith that He is here, and that He is in control.

"Now we see but a poor reflection as in a mirror;
then we shall see face to face."
(I Corinthians 13:12)

So there is a BIG picture going on. A MUCH bigger picture as we trust God in faith. As He freed the Hebrews from a cruel Pharaoh, so He will free you.

Look at this scripture, putting YOUR ABUSER'S NAME in place of the word "Egyptian." It helps to build our faith as we find refuge in God's ultimate victories.

"Therefore, say to the Israelites: 'I am the LORD, and I
will bring you out from under the yoke of _____.
I will free you from being slaves to them,
and I will redeem you with an outstretched arm
and with mighty acts of judgment.
I will take you as my own people, and I will be
your God.
Then you will know that I am the LORD your God, who
brought you out from under the yoke of _____.
And I will bring you to the land I swore with uplifted
hand to give to Abraham, to Isaac and to Jacob.
I will give it to you as a possession, I am the LORD."
(Exodus 6:6-8)

Grab hold of the truth in these verses; and, YES, they belong to you too!

"I will bring you out. . ."
"I will free you from being slaves. . ."
"I will redeem you with mighty acts of judgment."
"I will be your God."
". . .who brought you out from under the yoke. . ."
"I swore with uplifted hand" (a promise)

So as we make a decision to put our faith in God to lead our lives, He promises to give us all we need to rise above the suffering.

"He gives strength to the weary
and increases the power of the weak.
Even youths grow tired and weary,
And young men stumble and fall;
But those who hope in the LORD
Will renew their strength.
They will soar on wings like eagles;
They will run and not grow weary,
They will walk and not faint."
(Isaiah 40:29-31)

So can you look at yourself as a special product of God's creation? You are working through the immense suffering of domestic abuse. Wait on God and let him build your character in new and wonderful ways. He can make us fly like the eagle, soaring above all the turmoil, rising to new heights.

We may only see one piece of the jigsaw puzzle of our lives. The picture may not make sense to us. It's not complete. But it is God who completes the picture on the cover of the box. The BIG picture is clear to Him.

The goal is to become *"mature and complete, not lacking anything."* These tests of our faith produces PERSERVERANCE so that we can face anything this life has to offer. God has not left us alone and orphaned. The opposite is true. Just BELIEVE IT! God is your Father and He has promised to take care of us as beloved children. Suffering has a purpose, a deeper purpose, and He will make something GOOD out of it. Unbelievably, God says to rejoice in our sufferings as they give God a chance to work in our lives:

"Consider it pure joy, my brothers,
whenever you face trials of many kinds,
because you know that the testing of your faith
develops perseverance.

Perseverance must finish its work
so that you may be mature and complete,
not lacking anything."
(James 1:2-4)

"...that you may be mature and complete,
not lacking anything."
(James 1:2)

V. GOD RESTORES
Day 36: Returning a Blessing

The Golden Rule in Scripture says that we are to treat someone else in the same way that we want to be treated. As Jesus said:

"So in everything, do to others what you would have them do to you, for this sums up the Law and the Prophets."
(Matthew 7:12)

We are exhorted to treat others with kindness, no matter how they treat us. Does it seem hard to understand why ANYONE would disagree with this, and instead continually hurt someone else? What if that someone else is supposed to be the closest of friends—his wife? We are not expected to understand it, but we don't have to be a target of it. Nor do we follow that pattern in our own lives.

Jesus gave us a simple way to understand how we are to treat others. He said,

"Whatever you did for one of the least of these brothers of mine, you did to me."
(Matthew 25:40)

This verse says that when you are being hurt, it is like Jesus is directly being hurt. Jesus was not loved by everyone. In fact, He was *"despised and rejected of men"* (Isaiah 53:3) and eventually He was crucified on the cross by His enemies. That's how badly He was hurt. So He does understand suffering. You ask, "How could anyone ever hurt Jesus?" It is the picture of the evil world we are in.

It is with the power of the Holy Spirit that we are given the strength to overcome the evil in this world. We can address sin and do something about it. Sin does not have to rule over our lives.

One way to overcome evil is to return a blessing to all our contacts, whether they abuse us or not. Just return a blessing! God gives us this totally revolutionary way to live compared to the ways of the world. Instead of living in the darkness of hurt, he says we receive a blessing when we give a blessing to others. Here are some tips on how to do that:

"Finally, all of you, live in harmony with one another;
be sympathetic, love as brothers, be compassionate
and humble.
Do not repay evil with evil or insult with insult,
but with blessing, (emphasis mine)
because to this you were called so that you may
inherit a blessing."
(I Peter 3:8-9)

There are some more specific standards for us to live by:

"Whoever would love life
And see good days
Must keep his tongue from evil
And his lips from deceitful speech.
He must turn from evil and do good;
He must seek peace and pursue it.
For the eyes of the Lord are on the righteous
And his ears are attentive to their prayer,
But the face of the Lord is against those who do evil."
(I Peter 3:10-12)

The Lord even says that within our suffering, we can receive a blessing!

"Who is going to harm you if you are eager to do good?
But even if you should suffer for what is right, you are
blessed.
Do not fear what they fear; do not be frightened.
But in your hearts set apart Christ as Lord."
(I Peter 3:13-15)

In fact, we are admonished to actually BLESS those who hurt us.

"Bless those who persecute you;
bless and do not curse.
Rejoice with those who rejoice; mourn with those
who mourn.
Live in harmony with one another."
(Romans 12:14-16)

The definition of a "blessing" is to "make happy." God blesses us (or makes us happy) and we bless others (or make them happy). What a great way to live!

How do we "bless" someone who is our "abuser?" The truth is that an abuser cannot find it within himself to be happy. He is unhappy, with himself and the world. Only God can rescue him out of this despair. If you are a target of this abuse, the most you can do is be cordial and polite whenever you are together. And even that must be with caution as your kindnesses can be twisted into more hurt and confusion. Keep contacts minimal.

By returning kindness to an abuser, the Bible says that this in some way confronts his evil desires to hurt you. It's like heaping burning coals on his head.

"Do not repay anyone evil for evil.
Be careful to do what is right in the eyes of everybody.
If it is possible, as far as it depends on you,
live at peace with everyone.
Do not take revenge, my friends, but leave room
for God's wrath,
for it is written: 'It is mine to avenge; I will repay,'
says the Lord.
On the contrary: 'If your enemy is hungry, feed him;
If he is thirsty, give him something to drink.
In doing this you will heap burning coals on his head.'
Do not be overcome by evil, but overcome evil
with good."
(Romans 12:17-21)

What we do NOT do is retaliate, or return evil for evil, or hurl hurts back. As long as the abuser is treating you with a form of respect, your role is to be polite and gracious. But if the conversation starts to turn ugly, you are to immediately separate yourself. There are couples who have learned how to maintain some sort of a friendship, but it is rare in domestic abuse scenarios. For me when I have a common place to go with my former husband, he is polite to me at first, but then he can't seem to stop himself from making derogatory remarks. He has never repented of his sins against me, and still does not see them. But I see them, and I will not tolerate them anymore.

In some cases, sadly, the abuser NEVER stops finding ways to hurt you. In these cases, it may be better to have absolutely NO CONTACT. That's right! NO CONTACT! Holding on to the need to SEE the other person may not be advisable.

Some molds can never be broken, stuck in hard concrete. There's nothing more you can do. It may be the only way to stay in peace.

A few chapters in Romans give us insight about Christian conduct, or how to immerse ourselves in God's will to live in a peaceful and loving manner. Study Romans 12 – 16 to find a way to live with faith, hope and love. Here are some of the greatest truths for living the Christian life and the most practical help in all the New Testament. It will help us know how to conduct ourselves in social, civil and personal settings, and we don't have to stumble in the dark.

Above all, find ways to return blessings to others.

"...seek peace and pursue it" (I Peter 3:11).

V. GOD RESTORES
Day 37: Becoming Joyful

Me? Joyful? Isn't that a lot to ask after all I've been through? How can I just be "happy, happy?"

There were times I just couldn't feel it. In my past I had days and weeks and months (and sometimes years) of feeling afraid and alone. My life felt confused and I really couldn't be myself, or do what I wanted to do. Everything seemed to be falling apart, like walking a high wire with no net beneath me. My dreams were shattered, and I felt no hope for any positive change. And God wants me to be joyful? How does that work?

I will admit that this is a challenge for me. I am a very introspective person, thinking, thinking all the time. It's hard to let go and just have fun. I especially have a challenge when I wake up in the morning. For many mornings, I shared the first light of the sunrise with a husband that felt so insecure to me. What did THIS day hold for me? Now I am waking up alone, but some of the fears of the past can keep my spirit down. I confront these morning doldrums by turning to God as quickly as I can. I surrender the day to God and wait for Him to move in my life. By the end of the day, I feel thankful for all the wondrous things that happened. Especially that He lifted the cloud of darkness.

We can lose our joy when things don't meet our expectations. Our circumstances don't match up with our expectations. It's time to pause, breathe and set aside preconceptions. What did I EXPECT to happen? Surrendering the day to God can take away those expectations as your perspective now puts God in control. The day is not "bad" or "good," but moves in such a way that every encounter is programmed by God. I stay in His joy, His peace, and His hope. I joyfully say, "God is in charge."

God says, *"Rejoice in the LORD always. I will say it again: Rejoice!"* (Philippians 4:4)

Somehow the secret to true happiness is wrapped in this verse. It says, *"Rejoice IN THE LORD. . ."* There's something more to happiness than searching the earth to find it—with material possessions, with travels, with a big bank account, with a new wardrobe, with esteem and fame in the eyes of others. It is true that these things may be a part of our lives, but the real joy from God comes from within. After a day full of activity, we all put our head on the pillow at night with nothing but a cover. None of our material pursuits matter at that point. We are alone with our thoughts. It's what is in our hearts that matters. And we all die naked and bare, with nothing to claim but our heart and soul. That's what God sees, and that's all that matters. Do we feel peace in our hearts? Do we feel wrapped up in God's love? It's the condition of our heart that's all-important to God. So in all the busyness of life, God says to "Guard your heart" (Proverbs 4:23). The heart is the place that true character is formed. It alone holds the secrets of true success. Don't let anyone steal the precious gift of a God's richest blessings—love, joy, peace.

"The path of the righteous is like the first
gleam of dawn,
shining ever brighter
till the full light of day.
But the way of the wicked is like deep darkness;
They do not know what makes them stumble."
(Proverbs 4:18-19)

Guarding your heart means taking hold of our thoughts to live in the Light, not the darkness. It's all about redirecting our thinking patterns. God knows we have gone through some tough stuff. Focusing on God's purposes in life gives me a new direction and a new hope. In the beginning of this devotional, we talked about the fact that God *"rewards those who earnestly seek Him"* (Hebrews 11:6B). That's where deep joy is found.

This same scripture in Proverbs also gives us the SECRET to find true success in life:

"My son, pay attention to what I say;
listen closely to my words.
Do not let them out of your sight,
Keep them within your heart;
For they are LIFE (emphasis mine) *to those who find them*
And health to a man's whole body."
(Proverbs 4:20-22)

One secular song puts it this way: "Is that all there is? Then let's keep dancing." But God says there is more than the physical in this life. There is a deeper place to be, to find who we are in our core, and to draw close to Almighty God.

"Praise be to the God and Father of our Lord Jesus
Christ, who has blessed us in the heavenly realms
with every spiritual blessing in Christ."
(Ephesians 1:3)

That's what I want—*"every spiritual blessing in Christ."*

David in the Psalms expresses the range of his emotions, from deep sadness and despair to complete exultation. Reading the Psalms is a way to learn that these emotions are a part of the human condition. We can learn from David that there are times of weeping and times of rejoicing.

"Sing to the LORD, you saints of his;
praise his holy name.
For his anger lasts only a moment,
But his favor lasts a lifetime;
Weeping may remain for a night,
But rejoicing comes in the morning.
(Psalm 30:4-5)

David was in despair for many reasons. He committed adultery, he committed murder, he lost his firstborn son, and he was hunted by King Saul. Yet it is this same David who spent many hours alone with God as he watched the sheep out in the fields. As a young man he prayed and he sang praises to God with his harp. God eventually said about David that he was *"a man after my own heart"* (I Samuel 13:14). What a compliment! David was doing something RIGHT with his relationship to God. David did sin, but he then confessed his sin to God and sought forgiveness.

> *"To you, O LORD, I called;*
> *to the LORD I cried for mercy. . .*
> *Hear, O LORD, and be merciful to me;*
> *O LORD, be my help.*
> *You turned my wailing into dancing;*
> *you removed my sackcloth and clothed me*
> *with joy,*
> *that my heart may sing to you and not be silent.*
> *O LORD my God, I will give you thanks forever."*
> (Psalm 30:8; 10-13)

Finding that *"blessing in the heavenly realms"* only comes as we intentionally make steps to stay close to God as David did.

I want to suggest several practical things here that can help us get out of the doldrums and into a place of contentment. If we feel a cloud of darkness coming over us, we should recognize it for what it is, and then take some steps to eradicate it.

1. PINPOINT. Try to pinpoint what it was that brought your emotions down. Was it something someone said? Did you look at a picture that triggered some memories? Did you have a frightful dream? Did loneliness overwhelm you? Pinpoint it, so that you can confront it.

2. TAKE SOME ACTION. Deliberately do something that you KNOW makes you happy. For me, I put on some music or walk with my dog. Maybe you like some physical activity to release the tension. Maybe you call a friend or meet at a coffee shop for a good heart-to-heart talk. Maybe sitting down to write in your journal can help express your feelings.

3. NO SUBSTITUTES. Be wary of being sucked into some false avenues to release the inner pain. Alcohol doesn't do it, drugs don't do it.

Shopping doesn't do it, or splurging with money doesn't help. Spending the whole day playing Solitaire will not satisfy. Or spending the day in bed doesn't help take the pain away. Eating half the jar of peanut butter will not do it. None of these would be healthy choices. Call a friend if you feel tempted to stray into self-destructive activities.

4. TURN TO GOD'S WORD. Read the Psalms and find some comfort from God. Locate some verses that especially calm your soul and dwell on them. Sing some praise songs, or put on some relaxing CD's. Steady church attendance can also give God a chance to speak to you, and a chance for you to serve others. Serving others can bring you out of your introspective focus as you dwell on others.

5. TELL GOD. And finally, but actually first and foremost, tell God about the despair you are feeling. Be honest with God. Pour out your feelings, and then wait for Him to act on your behalf.

"'For I know the plans I have for you,' declares the LORD, 'plans to prosper you and not to harm you, plans to give you hope and future.

Then you will call upon me and come and pray to me,
And I will listen to you.
You will seek me and find me when you seek me with
all your heart.'"
(Jeremiah 29:11-13)

There's the key to lifting the burden of despair: "seek me with all your heart."

So I want to stress here that all of us need to do some sincere introspection. What is it that plunges us into despair, and what is it that can bring us out? And what can we do with God's guidance that can bring us to a peaceful place of contentment, no matter what?

". . .I have learned to be content whatever the
circumstances.
I know what it is to be in need,
And I know what it is to have plenty.
I have learned the secret of being content in any and
every situation,
Whether well fed or hungry,
Whether living in plenty or in want.
I can do everything through him who
gives me strength."
(Philippians 4:11-13)

Once your life was stifled and restricted. You felt some shame and guilt for just being yourself. People you trusted have turned their backs on you. Your husband has made it very hard for you to support yourself, so your life style is in a different place.

Look at yourself as a NEW CREATION. You are now free to be yourself. You can wake up with a purpose every day: serving God and serving others. Wait on God to reform you into the person you were meant to be. Face the fact that our experiences in life can keep our emotions bouncing, but the longer we walk with God the more contentment we will find as we see how He miraculously works in our lives. So take heart!

"We are hard pressed on every side, but not crushed;
perplexed, but not in despair;
persecuted, but not abandoned;
struck down, but not destroyed."
(2 Corinthians 4:8-9)

The best way to overcome the darkness is to focus on the BIG PICTURE God has created for us. There are reasons things happen, but God is the Deliverer with every hope for a bright future.

"For our light and momentary troubles are
achieving for us
an eternal glory that far outweighs them all.
So we fix our eyes not on what is seen,
But on what is unseen.
For what is seen is temporary,
But what is unseen is eternal."
(2 Corinthians 4:17-18)

The best way to walk through a day with a joyful and content spirit is to look passionately for God's blessings. Maybe it's in the morning sunrise, or the stars in the heavens. Maybe it is a flower blossoming, or the beauty of a light snowfall. Maybe it is the laughter of a child, or the sweet smile of a senior. Start the day with praise to God, and end it with heartfelt thanksgiving.

When worries or anxieties seem to pull you down, quote a scripture that reminds you of God's protective presence:

"Don't worry about anything;
instead, pray about everything.
Tell God what you need, and don't forget to thank Him
for His answers.

If you do this, you will experience God's peace,
which is far more wonderful than the human mind
can understand.
His peace will guard your hearts and minds
as you live in Christ Jesus."
(*The Living Bible*, Philippians 4:6-7)

"Rejoice in the Lord always, I will say it again:
Rejoice! Let your gentleness be evident to all.
The Lord is near."

(*The Living Bible*, Philippians 4:4-5)

V. GOD RESTORES
Day 38: Trusting God

I t may sound like an overworked cliché, to tell someone to "trust God." A victim of abuse has not had a good experience with trusting humans, and it may be difficult to trust God. What if God fails me too?

In addition to our inward feelings of doubt, we can't help but wonder if our most basic of human needs will be met. Will there be enough money for me to support my own needs? Food, clothes, shelter? Maybe your abuser has been the only income producer, and you feel a dependency on his provision. This is the one overwhelming single factor that prevents women from leaving men who are hurting them. They feel a hopeless dependency, and are filled with fear about a future on their own. The abuser knows this, and uses it to keep her subservient. Even saying, "you leave me and you are REALLY going to be broke." (True story!)

The truth is that a woman can become empowered to take care of herself. She may not be able to imagine being alone, but she CAN do it. It's not due to a feminist impetus to show the world how strong a woman is. Rather, it is the only option she has if she is to live in freedom, the freedom to be herself. She comes to the point that the abuse is restricting every part of her life, and she is living in hopeless trepidation. She MUST stop the sin of abuse.

She CAN get a new look at herself. The first thing to realize is that she is a woman created by God to do good works with her life. God is her "Controller," not another person. In a healthy human partnership, both individuals want the very best for each other. They support and bless each other as they each live out their gifts. They both live in submission to the will of God. And hurt has no part in this arrangement!

Jesus has said over and over that we CAN trust God for the basic needs of our lives. He says not to worry, that He will be there for us. It's a promise:

"And my God will meet all your needs according to his glorious riches in Christ Jesus."
(Philippians 4:19)

God may not answer our prayers in ways that WE think He should. But He WILL be there for us at every turn.

The truth is that God knows more about us than we know about ourselves. He knows what will REALLY bring us fulfillment in life. Our goals may not be His goals. Marriage? Riches? Employment? God said simply for us to look to Him. Jesus gives us the picture of the "birds of the air" and "the lilies of the field." God takes care of them:

> *"Do not worry about your life, what you will eat or*
> *drink; or about your body, what you will wear.*
> *Is not life more important than food, and the body*
> *more important than clothes?*
> *Look at the birds of the air; they do not sow or reap*
> *or store away in barns, and yet your heavenly Father*
> *feeds them.*
> *Are you not much more valuable than they?*
> *Who of you by worrying can add a single hour to*
> *his life?"*
> (Matthew 6:25 -27)

> *"And why do you worry about clothes?*
> *See how the lilies of the field grow.*

They do not labor or spin.

Yet I tell you that not even Solomon in all his splendor

was dressed like one of these."

(Matthew 6:28–29)

The secular world is consumed with soaking up earthly things. It's IMPORTANT to the "pagans" (as Jesus called them) so have the finest of foods, expensive drinks, the newest of homes, and the wardrobe of brand name clothing. Food, drink and clothes are basic needs. But in Jesus' world, they are of secondary importance to what is REALLY relevant:

"So do not worry, saying, 'What shall we eat?'

or 'What shall we drink?'

or 'What shall we wear?'

*For the **PAGANS** (emphasis mine) run after*

all these things,

and your heavenly Father knows that you need them.

But seek first his kingdom and his righteousness,

and all these things shall be given to you as well."

(Matthew 6:31-33)

This is part of what we discussed in the first section of this book: GOD LOVES YOU and GOD WILL TAKE CARE OF YOU.

Sorry to say that an abuse victim many times gets hung up with worry over her basic needs being met. It is not a time to be reckless, but God WILL supply your needs. In fact, her real needs are not for the physical as much as the emotional. She needs mostly to live her life without fear.

If an abused woman is planning to take a break from the relationship in order to seek assistance, she needs to make careful plans before jumping to a swift escape. The only exception is if the abuser gets lethal with a weapon, or if she has been wounded so badly that she needs the ER. If those two incidents occur, she CANNOT go back and must make a change.

But if she has time to plan her exit, she needs to find a "safe place" to go, save some money, think about potential work skills so that she can support herself, surround herself with professional, financial and legal support. Think carefully about what you expect in the relationship in order for the two of you to continue to live together. Things MUST change or you will not submit to this relationship again. Taking a break from the relationship is not a quick jump to divorce court.

It is a carefully planned exit to encourage a change in the relationship.

My escape was sudden and horrifying. After calling the sheriff and leaving with my dog, the doors of the house were locked shut (even with wooden planks nailed over the entrances). I left almost everything behind. He refused to divide up any of the possessions. My lawyer advised me to get the sheriff AGAIN and go back to get my stuff. I decided at that point to just leave it all behind. I don't need the furniture or the cans in the cupboard or the washer and dryer. It wasn't worth it to me. (My complete story can be found in my first book, *Surviving Domestic Abuse, with the Help of God* also by Ellis).

God has amazing and sometimes surprising ways to meet all our needs. On the day that I left under sheriff's protection, a waitress friend at a restaurant brought me a hot meal compliments of the kitchen. Since that day, I feel that God has astounded me with His love and care in MANY WAYS. I have never felt abandoned or forsaken. He is there!

One result is that I feel completely myself these days. After years of counseling and introspection, I feel stronger in myself. I feel braver. I feel unafraid. I feel free to develop my gifts as God gave them to me. I feel supported by the church. The most exciting thing is that I now have a mission and a purpose. I am devoted to helping other women in domestic abuse. I meet women frequently who need to talk. When I open up as a survivor, they open up to me. My goal (as in this book) is to point them God to restore their lives to wholeness.

So surround yourself with God's Word and remember how He has promised to care for you:

"Humble yourselves, therefore, under God's mighty hand, that he may lift you up in due time.

"Cast all your anxiety on him because he cares for you"
(I Peter 5:7).

V. GOD RESTORES
Day 39: Staying Healthy

Becoming healthy in our thinking and our behaviors toward others doesn't happen overnight. Once some new thinking has formed, staying healthy becomes the goal. Old patterns beg to repeat and repeat, and the danger is that they will be passed down the generations. Once that one link in the chain of abuse is broken, hopefully others will sit up and take notice. That chain needs to be smashed. One person in the family is standing up against destructive patterns. She may feel alone in her perceptions, mainly because family patterns are ingrained. Everyone is used to the negativity. But something is wrong here, and it needs to be fixed.

A revolution in our thinking comes with education and insight. The profiles of an abuser and of a victim are well established, but need to be learned. Overcoming these devastating behaviors takes counseling, prayer, and daily introspection with meditation on God's Word. The Word of God is the ultimate source about the WAY we should live.

Let's view a summary picture of the elements in a violent/abusive relationship from the "Power and Control Wheel" published by the National Center on Domestic and Sexual Violence. Power and control over another human being is revealed in a variety of scenarios:

- INTIMIDATION
  Making her afraid. Destroying property. Abusing pets. Displaying weapons.
- EMOTIONAL ABUSE
  Putting her down. Calling her names. Making her think she is crazy. Humiliating her.
- ISOLATION
  Controlling what she does, whom she sees and talks to, and where she goes. Limiting outside involvement.
- MINIMIZING
  Denying, blaming. Making light of the abuse, like it didn't happen. Saying she caused it.
- COERCION
  Making and/or carrying out threats to do something to hurt her. Threatening to leave her, commit suicide. Making her do illegal things.

- MALE PRIVILEGE
  Treating her like a servant. Making all the decisions. Being the one to define the roles of men and women.
- ECONOMIC ABUSE
  Making her ask for money. Preventing her from getting or keeping a job. Giving her an allowance. Not letting her know about or have access to family income.
- USING CHILDREN
  Making her feel guilty about the children. Using the children to relay messages. Using visitation to harass her. Withholding contact.

Some or all of these elements can be used by the batterer to establish and maintain control over his partner, and may lead to eventual physical or sexual assault.

The healthy relationship looks completely different and has the flavor of equality and respect.

- TRUST
  Supporting each other's goals in life. Respecting her right to her own feelings, friends, activities and opinions.
- NON-THREATENING

Talking and acting so that she feels safe and comfortable expressing herself and doing things.

- HONESTY

Accepting responsibility for self. Acknowledging past use of violence. Admitting being wrong. Communicating openly and truthfully.

- SHARED RESPONSIBILITY

Mutually agreeing on a fair distribution work. Making family decisions together.

- NEGOTIATION

Being fair. Seeking mutually satisfying resolutions to conflict. Accepting change. Being willing to compromise.

- RESPECT

Listening to each other non-judgmentally. Being emotionally affirming and understanding. Valuing each other's opinions.

- ECONOMIC PARTNERSHIP

Making money decisions together. Making sure both partners benefit from financial arrangements.

- RESPONSIBLE PARENTING

Sharing parental responsibilities. Being a positive, non-violent role model.

This list sounds great to me! When we look at the stark difference between the unhealthy and the healthy, it helps us to face the reality of the nature of our relationships. Are they healthy, or not? Are they partially healthy? We try to learn some new skills and make a willful decision to abandon the old patterns and develop qualities that are pleasing to God. Hopefully both partners can move toward healthy thinking and behaviors together. But if you have to do it alone, then do it alone. God is the only One we are living for.

"His divine power has given us everything we need for
life and godliness through our knowledge of him
who called us by his own glory and goodness.
Through these he has given us his very great and pre-
cious promises,
so that through them you may participate in the
divine nature and escape the corruption in the world
caused by evil desires."
(2 Peter 1:3-4)

We should strive for the healthy, in all our relationships. When I think of "unhealthy" from God's Word, I think of these acts of sin:

"The acts of the sinful nature are obvious;
sexual immorality, impurity and debauchery, idolatry
and witchcraft;
hatred, discord, jealousy, fits of rage, selfish ambition,
dissensions, factions and envy;
drunkenness, orgies, and the like.
I warn you, as I did before,
that those who live like this will not inherit the
kingdom of God."
(Galatians 5:19-21)

When I think of "healthy" from God's Word, I think of the fruit of the Spirit in this same passage:
"The fruit of the Spirit is love, joy, peace, patience,
kindness, goodness, faithfulness,
gentleness and self-control
Against such things there is no law."
(Galatians 5:22-23)

With an escape from an abuser, the true self of the victim has a chance to blossom. No longer is someone restricting her to be what HE wants her to be. She was a puppet on strings, with no say about herself. But those days are over.

In some ways it can be a scary thought, to answer only to yourself. An abuse victim is not used to this. She has enabled and supported her abuser, not only because he seemed stronger but also because that strength in some ways made her feel secure. Out of her lack of self-esteem, she was easily led. Naïve and gullible—that's what it is called.

When a victim starts concentrating on living a healthy life for herself, there will be no more false substitutes. She doesn't have to pretend anymore. She takes care of herself. Physically? She eats well, sleeps well, exercises well. Emotionally? She guards her spirit to stay balanced with emotional expression. Not too down, not too up! Spiritually? She has every freedom to walk with God without criticism.

One of the biggest new events is that she has finally found her "voice." She can speak for herself, and express her feelings. (This actually comes as shock for some people as the "new self" emerges from the "old self.") She can express her joys and her fears, her likes and her dislikes. She doesn't feel "forced" to do or not to do anything. She makes her own decisions.

Her personal connections seem to flourish—at home, at work, at church, in the neighborhood. It becomes easier to develop authentic friendships. She is free to help others when needed. She can make her own plans for outings with friends.

This daily development of the True Self means she has total acceptance of whom she is—created and loved by God. She can look at her imperfections with honesty, and earnestly seek God to continue molding her into the person she was created to be. She faces her faults and works on them so that she does not hurt herself or anybody else.

She feels safe, generous, authentic and free. The truth comes right from Jesus' own words:

> *"If the Son has made you free,*
> *you are free indeed."*
> (John 8:36)

With the indwelling Holy Spirit (*"love, joy, peace, patience, kindness, goodness, faithfulness, self-control"*) there is no way for abuse to invade and thrive. It just wouldn't be there. So stand firm on the truth of what it means to live with Christ in the center of our lives. Our words will show it, our actions will show it, our attitudes will show it, and our spirits will show it. We have been set free to be the person God wants us to be.

"Stand firm. Let nothing move you.
Always give yourselves fully to the work of the
Lord, because you know that your labor in the
Lord is not in vain."
(I Corinthians 15:58)

V. GOD RESTORES

Day 40: Being Still

It's time to be still. We have dwelled on living life God's way. We have embraced these truths:

God Made Me

God Loves Me

Abuse Hurts

God Heals Me

God Restores Me

If we believe these truths with all our hearts, then we are on the road to healing and recovery. It's time to sit on His lap and BE STILL.

"Be still and know that I am God." (Psalm 46:10)

That's where He wants us, and that's where we are.

What is it that tempts us to fall off His lap and return to negative patterns? Some things may plague us all of our lives, but not if we know how to confront them and become victorious over them. Satan is a thief, and he tries to steal from us what God wants to give us. He targets our joy, our peace, our hope. But HE CAN'T HAVE IT! He is a defeated enemy, and Christ is the Ruler of all.

We must also face the truth that God has given us a choice on how we live. All through the scriptures (almost on every page) there are examples of following God's ways, and disobeying God's ways. And that choice is the freedom we are given. The most graphic example of this choice is pictured with Jesus dying on the cross, two criminals crucified on either side. One rebuked and denied Him, hurling insults. The other man said, *"Remember me when you come into your kingdom."* And what a glorious response he received from Jesus:

> *"Jesus answered him, 'I tell you the truth,*
> *today you will be with me in paradise.'"*
> (Luke 23:39-43)

So there's the choice. Rebuke Him, or receive Him.

I want to testify to you that the only solid Truth for me is found in going God's way with all that I understand. Abandoning God's intervention in my life only results in all things bad. With Him in my life, I hear a strong message directed straight at me from His Word. As I digest scripture every day, I become the person He has really created me to be. And I'm always looking FORWARD.

Without Him? At this point I would be full of bitterness, retaliation, worry, anger, spitefulness, and hopefulness. I would be stuck in the mud of darkness and evil, only to eventually be buried in the quicksand. What kind of person would I be?

Since leaving my husband and earnestly seeking the Lord, I know I have become a new person, just like He promised. I watch myself for sin creeping in, and confess it immediately. I align myself with true values (God's values): honesty (the most important), truth, integrity, authenticity, joy, freedom. I listen to others, but I am not influenced by other's opinions of me. God is my only Judge, and I can trust Him! People can lead you astray, put negative ideas in your head, put expectations on you, manipulate you, and give totally wrong advice. I have several cherished counselors/friends and in our discussions, I match everything that is said to me with God's Word.

Countless times, COUNTLESS times, I have heard words of advice from friends, from counselors, from my pastor, from my Bible, etc., which become my "reality check" helping me stay on the path God has designed for me. I like to visualize myself in a big bubble. God has put me in there. He will let NOTHING pop my bubble of closeness to Him. If something makes an attempt to break me, I intentionally crawl back into His protective covering. I will not retaliate, I will not argue, I will not feel compelled to explain myself. I just simply will not ENGAGE. If assaults come, I remove myself and let God take care of it HIS way.

This is what it means to "take your burdens to the cross." The cross where Jesus died means He not only came to the earth to save me, but also to protect and care for me. Drop those burdens at His feet. He identifies with my grief, and He is there for me. I have been astounded over and over again HOW he has been there for me, but that is another book!

So let's make the decision to live in the TRUTH. Jesus never promised a life without trials. He just said He would be there for us through the trials.

"I do not give to you as the world gives.
Do not let your hearts be troubled
and do not be afraid."
(John 14:27)

In the world we see conflict on every side. We wake up every day to the news of wars and rumors of wars. Wars between nations, wars in our communities, and wars in our homes. But Jesus was speaking to our HEARTS, your internal self, your true self inside, your CORE. That's where peace is! We cannot get inner peace through our own efforts, but it comes by following God's ways.

How do we find His peace inside? Jesus says DON'T WORRY (*"Do not let your hearts be troubled"*) and DON'T FEAR (*"and do not be afraid"*). Those are two great tips. But the target of overcoming these temptations starts in the HEART. If worry or anger seems to plague your heart with unrest, pray OUTLOUD for the Lord God in heaven to calm your spirit.

Expect troubles as part of the world we are in. Simon Peter, the leader of Jesus' disciples, experienced difficulties as a follower. It helps me to see that Peter was in a spiritual battle as we are, but in the end, his life was mightily used by God.

"Simon, Simon, Satan has asked to sift you as wheat.
But I have prayed for you, Simon,
that your faith may not fail.
And when you have turned back, strengthen your
brothers."
(Luke22:31-32)

Take note of several facts here:

1. Satan was battling for Simon's soul and God allowed it.
2. Simon would be *"sifted like wheat"* or thrust into turmoil.
3. Jesus prayed for him.
4. Most important was that Simon's *"faith may not fail."*
5. Simon would turn back to Jesus.
6. As a result he would be in a position to *"strengthen your brothers."*

Maybe this was concerning the event when Peter denied Jesus to His face (Luke 22:54-62).

What a terrible place to be. Peter was caught in sin with Jesus looking directly at him. As a result of this experience and his repentance, Peter rose to a place with stronger faith. He became the authority figure of the early church after Jesus had ascended to heaven. His life is an example of the spiritual battle that we wrestle with every day.

Let's examine some things that might creep in to bring our hearts down. What makes us stressful and worried and sad? What captures our hope and our peace and our love? This is the battle that Satan uses:

ASKING WHY. We may look at other couples, seemingly happy, and wonder "why me?" Why doesn't my husband treat me like that? Why does he seem to get away with all kinds of evil, done in secret? Why doesn't God just zap him down?

ANSWER: Rather than asking "why?" maybe it would be better to ask "how?" How will God work in this life? There are no answers to "why?" Psychology might help, counselors might help, but we will never get a complete picture of why domestic abuse happens. Jesus said to "ask the right question."

"Walking down the street, Jesus saw a man
born blind from birth.
His disciples asked, 'Rabbi, who sinned:
this man or his parents?'
Jesus said, 'You're asking the wrong question.

You're looking for someone to blame.
There is no such cause-effect here.
Look instead for what God can do.'"
(MSG, John 9:1-3)

"LOOK INSTEAD FOR WHAT GOD CAN DO."

WORRY. I may wake up in the morning, not really knowing how my checkbook is going to balance. I'm wondering if I may have to move. What am I going to do on Christmas? Actually the worries can go on and on. What a "joy stealer!" Worry can be put in the category of "sin" because it simply means we do not trust God's promises.

ANSWER. Write down the promises of God as they are myriad throughout the scriptures! What promises do you need to hear? Write them down and post them on your mirror.

"His divine power has given us everything we need
for life and godliness
through our knowledge of him who called us
by his own glory and goodness.
Through these he has given us

*his very great and **precious promises***
(emphasis mine),
*so that through them you may participate in the
divine nature and escape the corruption in the world
caused by evil desires."*
(2 Peter 1:3-4)

RETALIATION. As we get stronger in ourselves, it can be very tempting to retaliate to someone who has hurt us so badly. We may do it in a quiet, passive aggressive way with one sarcastic word, or slander, or manipulation to cause distress. We can be stubborn or uncooperative, or do whatever we can to make his life difficult.

ANSWER: Step back and believe God when He says,

*"Do not take revenge, my friends,
but leave room for God's wrath, for it is written:
'It is mine to avenge; I will repay,' says the Lord."*
(Romans 12:19)

Turn it completely over to Him and trust Him to do what He says He will do. Don't let your thoughts stay in the darkness. Fill your mind with God's best.

"Finally, brothers, whatever is true, whatever is noble, whatever is right, whatever is pure, whatever is lovely, whatever is admirable—if anything is excellent or praiseworthy—think about such things."
(Philippians 4:8)

Each of us has our own list of how we can lose our joy in living this life with Jesus at our side. Pinpoint your greatest temptation and find ways to overcome it with God's help.

"Draw near to God, and He will draw near to you."
(James 4:8)

Now that we have worked our way through all the steps of recovery, let us find our rest at the foot of the cross. Jesus gave us EVERYTHING for a purposeful and meaningful life. In the end, the most precious words to hear will be:

"Well done, good and faithful servant."
(Matthew 25:21)

In eternity it will not matter how much money we leave behind, how many people knew us, how many places we have traveled, how big our house was, how long we were married, or how many times we went to church. It is our hearts that matters, and how we have lived for Him and Him alone.

"So we make it our goal to please him,
whether we are at home in the body or away from it.
For we must all appear before the judgment seat of
Christ, that each one may receive what is due him
for the things done while in the body,
whether good or bad."
(2 Corinthians 5:9-10)

The prophet Elijah struggled in the desert to know that God was with him. He was the only prophet left, standing alone in the wilderness, surrounded by enemies. The Lord fed him by sending ravens with food and giving him water from a nearby brook. But Elijah was afraid, hiding in a cave, longing for the Lord to rescue him.

And the Lord did appear to Elijah, just like he comes to us in his Spirit. We need to be looking for Him and longing for Him. It may not be in the way we think, but He WILL come.

For Elijah, he looked for God in a strong wind, in an earthquake, and in a fire. Strong things, but God chose something different. After the fire came a "gentle whisper" as the Lord was about to pass by. When all became quiet, the Lord spoke and Elijah heard. He got up from that place to serve God in wondrous ways. Read the whole story in I Kings 19.

So when all feels like you are at the end of yourself, if you feel, like Elijah, that you are alone and they are *"trying to kill"* you, if you fear for your next meal or for a drop of water on your tongue, if the future seems dark and uncertain, if you wonder if God is there at all, then take some time to sit in quiet before Him. The "ravens" are coming to feed you in whatever you need. The "brook" nearby will nourish your soul. He comes, but He may come in ways you never expected.

There is no limit to God's power and authority. The past may be engulfing you with doubts, but you can make the decision to commit the future to His control and His care. The sins of the past don't have to taint your life in the future.

No matter what somebody else does or does not do in your life, your solid commitment is to live a life pleasing to the Lord. Stand firm against sin and seek the righteousness and justice of the Lord. So dwell in His peace.

> *"The fruit of righteousness will be peace;*
> *the effect of righteousness will be quietness*
> *and confidence forever."*
> (Isaiah 32:17)

> **"Be still and know that I am God"**
> (Psalm 46:10).

V. GOD RESTORES

Prayer of God's Restoration

Father of Recovery, You have provided a way for us to
be Overcomers.
No matter what attacks us
In our bodies
In our emotions
In our minds
In our spirits,
You come with clarity and wisdom.
You show us the true path of life.
Though my body is hurting,
Though my mind feels in confusion,
Though my emotions are twisted,
You, Father, are my salvation.
Your Word makes me solid and complete.
There is no other place to find total healing
Because You heal my heart.
Your Word has said,
"Blessed is the man
Who does not walk in the counsel of the wicked,
Or stand in the way of sinners
Or sit in the seat of mockers.
But his delight is in the law of the LORD,
And on his law he meditates day and night"
(Psalm 1:1-2).
I praise you, LORD, for delivering me and being my
Delight.
Amen

Conclusion

We have reached the end of our 40 days of earnestly seeking the Lord. That doesn't mean that we are now perfectly healed and restored. In fact, it might be a good idea to start all over in this devotional to solidify some sound thinking about our lives. Hopefully, as time goes by, we can become more and more transformed in our minds as we seek God's will— *"his good, pleasing and perfect will"* (Romans 12:2).

Let's review the main points that are part of our transformation:

God Created YOU. God made you just as you are. He doesn't pick favorites. He has not forgotten you. He has not abandoned you. He created you from the very beginning in your mother's womb, and He loves you with an everlasting love. You may have a hard time understanding all that has happened to you, but God has a future and a hope for you, despite the trials of life. Be thankful that God created you, just as you are!

God Loves YOU. Each one of us is unique. You are God's workmanship. He has given each of us certain gifts and talents, and we can use them in His service. The greatest fulfillment in life comes from developing and using all of our gifts for the work of the Lord. He has special things that only YOU can do. You are important to God in every single day of your life. God wants to fill you with his Holy Spirit so that the fullness of your being can come out in service to others. God is glorified as you live your life out of love for Him. Be thankful for His great love for you!

Abuse Hurts YOU. It is not God's will for you to be the target of abusive acts which can come in many forms—verbal, emotional, physical, spiritual. All abuse is meant to disable you, to destroy your confidence and make you dependent on your abuser. Because of a personality disorder, the abuser has a need to control someone weaker than himself, which gives him a sense accomplishment. He feels inadequate and inferior in himself, and controlling another human being brings a feeling of power. He leans on his victim, hanging on for dear life, as she gives his life some purpose and meaning. If she dares to step away in any form (arguing back, hitting back, leaving the premises, etc.), or stand up to him directly, his anger can become out of control. It is not a safe place for the victim or for the abuser. The bottom line is that violence against another is sin, and it must be stopped. Recognize abuse as SIN!

God Heals YOU. God knows and understands what you are going through. Jesus on earth experienced the extreme of abuse as He was tortured and nailed to a cross. He knows what it means to be "despised and rejected" of men. Jesus came to rid our lives of the control of sin. He is the great Healer. As we turn to him to find forgiveness for our own sins, he also gives us guidance on how to live in His love, His joy and His peace. As He forgives us, we can forgive others. He can guide us out of a dysfunctional and purposeless life, into a life rich in blessings from Almighty God. He can heal our hearts, and bring us to a safe and protected place. Be thankful for His healing power.

God Restores YOU. With God's power, our lives can be renewed and restored. He can bring healing to a tortured marriage when both husband and wife humbly fall on their knees and ask for His cleansing of sin and His guidance. Jesus IS *"the way, the truth and the life"* and He is more than willing to show us

THE WAY to a positive relationship. Some abusers come, and other abusers don't. Whether he comes or not, you are committed to living life as God intended, in obedience to Him. There is no abuse in that life! Staying close to the Word of God, either in personal study or with a support group, is essential in finding the true path in life. Each of us needs to make our own decision to follow Christ and live as one of His disciples. If both husband and wife turn humbly to Christ for healing in their dysfunction, there is a good probability that their marriage can be restored. But if only one of the two wants to live in God's Light, there will only be continued difficult times. Coming out of denial and following the ways of Christ will restore what has been devastated, either for both husband and wife, or maybe only one. Be thankful that God has the power to restore your life to fullness!

In all the despair of life, God wants us to turn to Him and silently trust Him to work His wonders in our lives:

"Be still and know that I am God."

(Psalm 46:10)

A contemporary song by Ed Cash brings some comfort as we put ourselves in God's hands:

"When the waves rise against me
and the wind tries to draw me away
I will stand on the mountain,
Safe in Your arms I will sing

He is here for the broken
And the life to the one who is undone
He is peace to the wounded
And hope for the helpless one.

He is here, He is here.
Be still my soul, be still
Be still my soul, be still
Wait patiently upon the Lord
Be still my soul, be still."

V. GOD RESTORES

Psalm 91

He who dwells in the shelter of the Most High
Will rest in the shadow of the Almighty.
I will say of the LORD, 'He is my refuge and
My fortress,
My God, in whom I trust.'

Surely he will save you from the fowler's snare
And from the deadly pestilence.
He will cover you with his feathers,
And under his wings you will find refuge;
His faithfulness will be your shield and rampart.

You will not fear the terror of night,
Nor the arrow that flies by day;
Nor the pestilence that stalks in the darkness,
Nor the plague that destroys at midday.

A thousand may fall at your side,
Ten thousand at your right hand,

But it will not come near you.
You will only observe with your eyes
And see the punishment of the wicked.

If you make the Most High your dwelling—
Even the LORD, who is my refuge—
Then no harm will befall you,
No disaster will come near your tent.

For he will command his angels concerning you
To guard you in all your ways;
they will lift you up in their hands,
So that you will not strike your foot against a stone.
You will tread upon the lion and the cobra;
You will trample the great lion and the serpent.

'Because he loves me,' says the LORD, 'I will
Rescue him;
I will protect him, for he acknowledges
My name.
He will call upon me, and I will answer him;
I will be with him in troubles,
I will deliver him and honor him.
With long life will I satisfy him
And show him my salvation.'"

A Hymn of God's Shelter

"Under His wings
I am safely abiding.
Though the night deepens
And tempests are wild.
Still I can trust Him
I know He will keep me.
He has redeemed me
And I am His child.

Under His wings, under His wings.
Who from His love can sever?
Under His wings
My soul will abide.
Safely abide forever."
—William Cushing (1823-1902)

"If you hold to my teaching,
you are really my disciples.
Then you will know the truth,
And the truth will set you free. . .

So if the Son sets you free,
You will be free indeed."

John 8:31b-32; 36

Appendix

How to Organize A
Domestic Abuse Alliance Group
In your Church

* * * * * *

Domestic Abuse Alliance (DAA)

Organizing a Program at Your Church

The church should be on the front lines of defending the defenseless, advocating for the abused, soothing the hurting. God's Word shows us the standard:

"The Spirit of the Sovereign Lord is on me,
because the LORD has anointed me
to preach good news to the poor.
He has sent me to bind up the brokenhearted,
To proclaim freedom for the captives
And release from darkness for the blind,
To proclaim the year of the LORD's favor
And the day of vengeance of our God,
To comfort all who mourn,

And provide for those who grieve in Zion—
To bestow on them a crown of beauty
Instead of ashes,
The oil of gladness
Instead of mourning,
And a garment of praise
Instead of a spirit of despair. . ."
(Isaiah 61:1-3)

"Live in peace with each other.
And we urge you, brothers,
warn those who are idle,
encourage the timid,
help the weak,
be patience with everyone."
(I Thessalonians 5:13b-14)

The mandate is clear: "*bind up the brokenhearted."* Sadly, the church has become far too silent, far too distant, far too impotent in addressing domestic abuse. Why? Domestic abuse is not supposed to happen in the church. However, I am one who can testify that I was a woman, sitting next to my husband in church, with his arm draped around my shoulders, not speaking a word to anyone about the truth in our home—I was besieged by abuse and terror, confusion and recklessness.

How can the church open up to become a needed voice in failing marriages due to devastating relationships at home? The reality needs to come out, and not kept secret. A victim of domestic abuse finds it extremely difficult to tell ANYONE what is happening in her home. She's embarrassed, humiliated, fearful about the future, and not finding a listening ear.

I am thankful to Messiah United Methodist Church, Plymouth MN, which came alongside me in my despair and weakness after escaping a violent relationship. With the strong support of the pastor (Steve Richards), I not only found acceptance and compassion, but was also able to create a ministry for the abused at the church. These are the results! This is how we organized and how we function in this new ministry.

First, it is important to clearly recognize two things: what we are, and what we are not called to do.

What We Are Not

Our role needs to be clearly understood.

1. **We are not counselors**. Domestic abuse is a very complex dynamic and only educated professionals are equipped to give therapy. We can

offer support with the Word of God, but leave the big therapy to the professionals in the field.

2. **We are not police**. Our role is not to storm a home, or bring accusations against any party. We are not the ones to confront an abuser. We are not to take sides.

3. **We are not social workers**. Most churches are not equipped to deal with basic needs, like housing, food, clothing. We may understand that basic needs must be met, but there are resources in most every community to deal with homelessness, financial crisis, job searches. It is imperative that we become aware of the resources in the community, and become a referral agent.

4. **We are not running a hotel for the abused**. It is not expected that the homeless victims will move into the home of church members. There are resources for emergency housing in nearly every community.

5. **We are not the bank.** Advocates are not expected to donate funds to individuals in need. The church may choose to form a Rescue Fund designated for emergency situations. One of the first practical things an abused woman

needs is some cash for daily needs. The church can provide temporary help, but again the professional organizations in the community will be able to meet monetary needs.

6. **We are not the judge.** Only a judge can issue a restraining order. We can give the victim support in finding a "safe place" but it is not our place to take the action of assisting an escape. Again in real life a judge listens to BOTH sides before determining an outcome. Our role is merely to be compassionate and supportive to both the abuser and the abused. We are the path to receiving help, and we encourage both parties to engage in Bible reading and prayer with a supportive group.

What We Are

We are simply a CONDUIT in order to direct victims to practical assistance.

Then what is our role in the church?

1. We make the public aware of the resources available in reaching out to the abused.

2. We take time to talk with victims, one on one. (This is the most important thing in this ministry—talking one on one.)

3. We conduct a Bible study targeting the issues of abuse. (This book, *The Shelter,* would be an excellent resource in searching the Scriptures on this issue.)

4. We commit to praying for every person in abuse—both the victim and the abuser.

5. We are aware of domestic violence resources in the community—shelters, legal advice, counselors, etc. We take every opportunity to make this information public, and lead those in need to find some professional help.

6. We understand that doing an intervention in an unhealthy marriage can take weeks, months, years. We are not in fulltime work, but we are available as much as possible. This step is called being "faithful" to the long-term ministry.

7. We counsel using the Word of God, not our own ideas. We refer the hurting individuals to professional counselors. (Some counselors are more equipped to deal with domestic abuse than others. Approved counselors should be screened.)

8. We take advantage of October Domestic Abuse Awareness Month. A table could be placed in the foyer of the church with brochures, books,

and other information about domestic abuse. An advocate could stay at the table to answer questions (and seek out those who are in need of help).

9. The church could be challenged to give financial support for specific items, such as diapers, gas cards, toiletries, clothes, etc. Take a collection of designated monies during the Domestic Abuse Awareness month, October. (One package of diapers; a gas card, etc.)

Realize that not EVERYONE in the church is called to this ministry. It can start with just two people, but hopefully the pastor and church staff will endorse the ministry.

How Is It Organized?

I. CREATE A CORE GROUP

A. Search for a core group of people in the church who would like to commit to this ministry. The pastor or church staff should interview each member of the core group to determine the motivation for joining this   ministry. One person can be the designated leader. It should not be necessary to meet often, maybe once a month.

(Note: This group should NOT be the platform for victims to retaliate, or vent grudges, or tell repeated stories. The goal is to help others, by looking FORWARD.)

B. Make a plan for outreach. This ministry should find a way to become visible in the church—promotion cards, bulletin announcements, web site contact information, occasional brief speaking opportunities in the church fellowship, emergency cards available in the women's restroom, etc. Include contact information.

C. Each member of the core group must sign a Contract of Confidentiality. (A sample contract is included.) Because women coming out of abuse have a very difficult time TRUSTING anyone, this group MUST be committed to confidentiality.

II. MINISTER TO THE ABUSED

A. Create a weekly, bi-weekly, or even monthly open advocacy group meeting. It is a publicized place for anyone to have a "drop in" visit. Each individual is listened to, and comforted with Scripture and prayer. Remember that this is a HUGE step for an abused woman, to tell someone her "secret." Again, this devotional book, *The Shelter,* would be an excellent resource for a targeted Bible study concerning domestic abuse.

B. Promote a 24-hour phone rescue. It could be a rescue organization in your community, or simply a phone number of a contact person in the church.

C. Meet one-on-one with each victim as everyone's story is different, although also the same in many ways. The victim must feel safe, and in a trusted partnership. Once the individuals in the core group are made visible in the church, many private conversations can come up at any time. The core group will be viewed as safe people to talk to. Always be READY. Your conversation may be a vital one!

D. Be aware that it takes an enormous step of courage for a woman to come out of the darkness and share her frightening situation. She is not only apprehensive about the consequences of confronting her abuser, but she may not want to "disrupt" the family system, even if it is a destructive one. Basically, she is usually filled with fear about making any changes.

For this reason, do not make snap emotional decisions. Her safety as is of utmost importance, as well as the safety of her whole family. Make decisions only after consulting with others in the core group and/or knowledgeable professionals.

Why does the church need to become actively involved? We have the way to find forgiveness, reconciliation, and restoration. With Jesus in the center, healing and recovery can come. A reluctant abuser should be prayed for. God must do the work in his inner core before there is recovery.

Let's do it, church! Help the helpless, encourage the weak, and as Jesus said, "feed my sheep" (John 21:17), especially those who are suffering.

Domestic Abuse Alliance (DAA)

Contract of Confidentiality

As a member of the Domestic Abuse Alliance ministry, I understand:

I. The Purpose
A. To minister to individuals caught in domestic abuse (mental, physical, emotional, spiritual).

B. To become an advocate by making resources readily available within and without of the church.

C. To meet together as the DAA group dedicated to organizing the church's specific ministry to the abused.

D. To support and promote the domestic abuse organizations in the community.

E. To search the Bible for supportive scriptures.

F. To pray for all individuals involved, both the abuser and the abuser.

G. To continually pursue knowledge about the dynamics of domestic abuse.

H. To find ways to raise financial support when needed (i.e., donations, fundraisers, etc.)

II. Things to Avoid

A. Counseling. Professional counselors are needed as part of a therapeutic recovery. The DAA group only advises with the Word of God.

B. Social Worker. Community resources have the ways and means to deal with immediate personal needs (i.e. shelter, food, money, legal advice, financial advice, etc.).

C. Police work. It is the role of law enforcement to make an approach in confronting an abuser, as it is a dangerous place for the victim. Police make the enforcement decisions, while the group is committed to prayer.

D. Hotel. It is not expected that the group provide shelter for the abused. Again, community resources are equipped to deal with emergency housing.

E. Bank. Group members are not expected to supply monetary assistance. Emergency funds could be made available through the church. Fundraisers could help to supply this resource.

F. Judge. We are to love and support both the abuser and the abused, without "taking sides." We are not the judge and jury.

III. The Pledge

A. I pledge to faithfully support the Domestic Abuse Alliance group by attendance, phone calls, promotion, etc.

B. I pledge to be completely and totally confidential within the members of the DAA group.

C. I pledge to be a mandated reporter to law enforcement if awareness is clear that an individual is in dire danger. The DAA group should discuss this step before any action is initiated.

D. I pledge to use my resources to build this ministry in the church with on-going promotion.

E. I pledge to be open to conversations by prospective individuals who are gradually working their way out of a violent environment. Outreach usually starts with one-on-one conversations.

F. I pledge to attend/lead the Bible study group that is offered weekly, bi-weekly, or monthly at the church with a focus on domestic abuse.

G. I pledge to pray for God's intervention in destructive families.

Signed_____ Date_____

Church_____ Pastor_____

"The Spirit of the Sovereign Lord is on me,
because the LORD has anointed me
to preach good news to the poor.
He has sent me to bind up the brokenhearted,
To proclaim freedom for the captives
And release from darkness for the
Prisoners,
To proclaim the year of the LORD's favor
And the day of vengeance of our God,
to comfort all who mourn,
And provide for these who grieve in Zion—to bestow
on them
a crown of beauty
instead of ashes,
The oil of gladness

Instead of mourning,
And a garment of praise
Instead of a spirit of despair." (Isaiah 61:1-3).

Additional book
by the author, Ellis.

Surviving Domestic Abuse

With the Help of God

The personal story of the author, Ellis, and how she finally escaped from domestic abuse domination. She details how her early life prepared the way, how she was easily duped by an abuser, and how she finally recognized the devastating environment she was in. She details what she has learned about the Profile of an Abuser, which is commonly similar. Her eventual escape gives wisdom and guidance in how to confront domestic abuse safely.

Her goal in telling her story is to strengthen others battling the same issues. God's Word speaks strongly against sin, and God is there to strengthen those who stand up against sin, and live in His Light. Today she is a speaker on the subject, and can be contacted through Xulon Press. (She must keep her real identity secret because of unknown consequences.)